MHQ:
The
Quarterly
Journal
of Military
History

Winter 2002
Volume 14, Number 2

A guerrilla prepares to throw a grenade, in a 1943 poster intended to inspire
Americans by reminding them of the Filipinos' struggle against their Japanese occupiers.
Beginning on page 56, John W. Whitman points out that the Filipino guerrillas' most
important contribution to Allied victory was not fighting the Japanese but
rather gathering and transmitting intelligence about them (Corbis).

A NOTE TO OUR READERS

A sound grounding in military history should provide a person with certain advantages over those who lack such knowledge. For example, you would expect a military historian to be better able to accurately define an ongoing military-related event as an historic turning point than someone who had little familiarity with military history. In other words, untrained participants in an episode or novice contemporary observers are at a disadvantage when compared to the educated participant or observer. After all, historians spend much of their time determining that occurrence A caused outcome B and that A was therefore a turning point or pivotal event.

I recall being at the Federal Bureau of Investigation's field office in Washington, D.C., late on a Friday afternoon in 1981 while one of the twentieth century's great turning points was dawning. My task there involved a closed-door session with the bureau's special agent in charge (SAC) of the Capitol District. Business concluded, the agent offered to escort me through his domain on my way out. Most of his personnel were departing for the weekend as I was briefed on the function of various departments at each of the four floors on our way down to the building's lobby. However, at one stop, the floor containing a number of sections dealing with surveillance of Soviet bloc embassies in Washington, no one was leaving and the atmosphere was near pandemonium. Everyone there seemed to be excited, and most were hurriedly talking on the phone. The SAC was as mystified as I was.

After a hushed conversation with the section supervisor, the SAC turned to me with a broad smile and said that during the last hour, the crackdown on the Solidarity movement begun that morning in Poland had resulted in rapidly growing numbers of Polish diplomats seeking asylum in the United States. He remarked that the phone calls were being made from pay phones all over the District of Columbia. The SAC informed me that his agents were giving defection instructions but were eagerly pointing out to the callers the advantages of remaining in Polish government service while secretly working for the United States.

The thought flashed through my mind that I was witnessing the beginning of the end of the Cold War. If Polish emissaries were switching sides, what about the Polish army? Poland not only occupied a crucial piece of geography, its army—the largest of Eastern Europe's armed forces—was the linchpin of the Warsaw Pact. Reaching the lobby, I distinctly remember deciding that great change was unlikely. If there was a revolt in Poland, the Soviet armed forces would undoubtedly put it down if the Polish army failed to do so.

I was wrong. I now believe it was the dissolution of the Marxist government in Warsaw, and not the oft-claimed American military buildup during that decade, that initiated the collapse of the Communist coalition. Historians may be better able to define the factors that might contribute to a pivotal event, but they are no better than anyone else in spotting a turning point as it occurs.

MHQ: The Quarterly Journal of Military History / Winter 2002

A **PRIMEDIA** Publication

Editor
Rod Paschall

Associate Editor
Richard G. Latture

Senior Editor
Joseph L. Bageant II

Consulting Editor
Christopher J. Anderson

Copy Editor
Claudia Gary Annis

Photo and Art Research Manager
Gina McNeely

Photo and Art Researcher
Kate Lewin/Paris

Photo and Art Research Assistant
Annette V. Kiesow

Editorial Director
Roger L. Vance

Managing Editor
Carl von Wodtke

Assistant Managing Editor
Nan Siegel

Creative Director
Barbara Sutliff

Art Director
Marty Jones

Editorial Production Coordinator
Beverly D. Frye

Editorial Production Assistant
Deborah L. Bennett

Editorial Resources Coordinator
Shirley Bailey

Editorial Assistant
Kathy E. Groves

Editorial Consultant
Robert Cowley

Contributing Editors
Stephen E. Ambrose, Caleb Carr, David G. Chandler,
Theodore F. Cook, Haruko Taya Cook, Arther Ferrill,
Thomas Fleming, Victor Davis Hanson, Alistair Horne,
Samuel Hynes, David Kahn, John Keegan,
Paul Kennedy, Richard H. Kohn, David Clay Large,
Jay Luvaas, John A. Lynn, William McNeill,
Allen R. Millett, Williamson Murray, Geoffrey Norman,
Robert L. O'Connell, Geoffrey Parker, H. Darby Perry,
Douglas Porch, John Prados, Willard Sterne Randall,
Elihu Rose, Stephen W. Sears, Dennis E. Showalter,
Al Silverman, Ronald H. Spector, Geoffrey C. Ward

Associate Group Publisher
Joseph Lyons

Business Manager
Darin Wolfe

New Business Manager, Circulation
Mark Fleetwood

Associate Publisher
Dean Regan

Lead Production Manager
Karen G. Gardner

Lead Production Planner
Karen M. Bailey

PRIMEDIA Inc.
Chairman & CEO Tom Rogers
President & Director Charles G. McCurdy
Vice Chairman Beverly C. Chell

PRIMEDIA Consumer Media & Magazine Group
President & CEO John Loughlin
Chief Operating Officer Daniel E. Aks
Executive VP, Consumer Marketing/ Circulation Steven Aster
Senior VP/Chief Financial Officer Linda C. Jenkins
Senior VP, Mfg., Production & Distribution Kevin Mullan
Senior VP, Human Resources Kenneth P. Slivken
VP/CIO, Information Technology Armand Madeo
VP, Database & Consumer Information John DePalm
VP, Single Copy Sales Thomas L. Fogarty
VP, Business Development Corinne Helman

PRIMEDIA History Group
Senior VP, Publishing Director Tom Rice
VP, Publishing Director Brent Diamond
VP, Consumer Marketing David Ball
VP, Production Dominick P. Elsener
VP, Manufacturing Budgets & Operations Lilia Golia

PRIMEDIA

NATIONAL PORTRAIT GALLERY/ SMITHSONIAN INSTITUTION/ART RESOURCE, NY

Cover: Winston Churchill wears his honorary air commodore's uniform, in Douglas Chandor's 1946 portrait. Beginning on page 20, Williamson Murray explains that Churchill waged a 1930s campaign to rearm Britain before leading it through WWII.

Back cover: Flames engulf *La Cordelière* during her battle with the English fleet. The story of Henry VIII's first naval war begins on page 38 (Bibliothèque Nationale).

MHQ: The Quarterly Journal of Military History (ISSN 1040-5992) is published quarterly by PRIMEDIA Enthusiast Group. The known office of publication is: 741 Miller Drive SE, Suite D-2, Leesburg, VA 20175. Periodical postage paid at Leesburg, VA, and additional mailing offices. Postmaster: Send subscription information and address changes to: *MHQ*, P.O. Box 420235, Palm Coast, FL 32142-0235. Single copies: $17.99. Yearly subscriptions in U.S.: $69.95; Canada: $79.95; Foreign: $89.95 (in U.S. funds only). *MHQ* neither endorses nor is responsible for the content of advertisements in its pages. Copyright 2001 by PRIMEDIA Enthusiast Group, Inc., a PRIMEDIA Company, all rights reserved. The contents of this magazine may not be reproduced in whole or in part without consent of the copyright owner. *MHQ* is a registered trademark of PRIMEDIA Enthusiast Publications, Inc.

All articles published in *MHQ* are rigorously fact-checked. References for a particular article may be obtained by sending a stamped, self-addressed envelope to our editorial offices. Selected articles are abstracted and indexed in *Historical Abstracts* and *America: History and Life.*

Subscription Information:
U.S./Canada: (800) 829-3340
Foreign Subscribers: (386) 447-6318
Back Issues: (800) 358-6327•(201) 840-4822 (foreign)
Reprint Information: Bill Breidenstine (717) 540-6722
(717) 540-6727 (fax)

PRINTED IN THE U.S.A.
Canadian Sales Agreement #1226010
Canadian GST #R123452781

Viewed from the ruins of the Temple of Apollo, it is easy to see why Acrocorinth's precipitous limestone cliffs made the height an obvious site for imposing fortifications. Forces of the Cypselid dynasty probably built the citadel's first walls, as early as 600 B.C. (Photography by Jefferson M. Gray unless otherwise noted).

Citadel of Greek Legend

Perched above the Isthmus of Corinth, Acrocorinth witnessed more than two millennia of sieges, attacks, insurgencies, and mighty intrigues.

by Jefferson M. Gray

Rising sharply some eighteen hundred feet from the coastal plain behind the ruins of ancient Corinth is a dome-shaped limestone mass—Acrocorinth. Its walls have seen the passing occupations of classical Greeks, Macedonians, Romans, Byzantines, Frankish Crusaders, Ottoman Turks, Venetians, and the soldiers of the reborn Greek nation. It was fought over from the early classical era through the mid-nineteenth century. One of its legendary sieges inspired an opera by Gioacchino Rossini. Another was celebrated in an epic poem by Lord Byron.

Much of the durable fortress' importance in history is due to its strategic location a few miles west of the narrow Isthmus of Corinth that connects northern Greece and the Peloponnesus. Corinth began as a prosperous trading center near the land bridge separating the Corinthian and Saronic Gulfs well before 1000 B.C. The first walls around Acrocorinth's summit were probably built by the strongmen of the tough, commercially oriented Cypselid dynasty, which ruled Corinth in the seventh and sixth centuries B.C. The summit was already encircled by high walls and massive towers when Philip II of Macedon, the father of Alexander the Great, seized and garrisoned Acrocorinth following his shattering victory at Chaeronea in 338 B.C. over the central and southern Greek city-states. The front portion of the massive tower that frames the right side of the third inner gateway probably dates to Philip's time or before.

In the century after Alexander's death in 323 B.C., Acrocorinth became a powerful rook on the chessboard of Greek international politics as the restless states of central and southern Greece struggled to reclaim their independence from Macedon. Acrocorinth's steep cliffs and high walls made it practically impregnable to conventional assault. But it proved less secure against opponents employing guile or stealth. On two occasions a few years apart in the second half of the third century, the citadel fell to opponents whose cunning recalled that of Sisyphus, the best known of Corinth's semilegendary kings.

During the middle of the third century B.C., Corinth and the island of Euboea were part of the realm of Antigonus II Gonatus, king of Macedon, and were ruled as an appanage by his nephew, Alexander. But Antigonus' trust in his nephew was misplaced. In 253 B.C., Alexander revolted, declared himself an independent monarch, and seized most of the Macedonian fleet while it was laid up in Corinthian ports for the winter. He then formed a diplomatic alliance with his uncle's bitter enemy, Ptolemy II of Egypt.

After the loss of his fleet, Antigonus was powerless to retaliate against his nephew. But he yearned—both for strategic and emotional reasons—to recover Corinth, where he had spent much of his youth. The historian Plutarch later recorded that the old king was "continually occupied with devising how to take it by surprise from those that were then masters of it, since he despaired to do so by open force."

For five years, Antigonus bided his time. Then in 248 B.C., Alexander died, leaving his queen, Nicaea, to rule his principality. The aging but shrewd Macedonian monarch offered Alexander's middle-aged widow the chance to marry Demetrius, his young, handsome son. Nicaea jumped at the opportunity. The nuptials were set to be celebrated at Corinth in 247 B.C. Nicaea did not totally succumb to romantic fantasies, however. She prudently maintained a strong garrison in Acrocorinth when Antigonus, Demetrius, and their attendants arrived.

The Macedonian king seemed untroubled by Nicaea's precautions. Upon arriving in Corinth, Plutarch recorded, Antigonus beguiled the queen and the citizens with daily entertainment and banquets "as one that had nothing else in his mind but to give himself up for a while to indulgence in pleasure and mirth." One evening, as the nuptial day approached, Nicaea set off for the theater in a richly decorated sedan chair, with Antigonus—short, snub-nosed, and knock-kneed but still vigorous at seventy-three—walking in apparently solicitous attendance at her side. Their party soon reached a fork where one road ran down to the theater and another turned sharply uphill to Acrocorinth. Calling out to Nicaea to continue without him, Antigonus and the men of his personal guard hung back until she passed from sight. Then, "bidding farewell to the music, farewell to the wedding," Antigonus raced uphill "faster than one would have thought his age would have permitted" until he and his men stood outside Acrocorinth's main gate.

Antigonus pounded on the gate with his staff and demanded entry. Many of the members of the citadel's garrison had slipped away to enjoy the festivities, and those who remained were apparently befuddled by too much celebratory wine. They opened the gate, and the Macedonian monarch and his men quickly seized the citadel. After that, there was no more talk of

Nicaea marrying Demetrius, but the aged king now had his own reasons to celebrate. As Plutarch recorded, "Having thus made himself master of the place, he could not contain himself for joy; but though an old man, and one that had seen many turns of fortune, he reveled in the open streets and in the midst of the market-place, crowned with garlands and attended with flute-women, inviting everybody he met to partake in his festivity."

Fortune, however, still had further tricks to play on Antigonus, who was destined to hold Acrocorinth for only four years. In the adjoining city-state of Sicyon lived a man whose obsession with Acrocorinth matched that of Antigonus himself. Aratus, Sicyon's leading statesman, was the commanding general of the Achaean League, a military coalition composed of Sicyon and

Background: Acrocorinth's Second Gate, which was rebuilt by the Venetians after an earlier structure was destroyed in 1458 by fire from the massive cannons of Mehmet II, a ruthless Ottoman sultan. Inset: The remains of the thirteenth-century Frankish castle erected atop Acrocorinth's southwestern ridge.

other Greek states of the northern Peloponnesus. He dreamed of seizing Acrocorinth for the Achaean League, thereby liberating Corinth from nearly a century of foreign rule and sealing off Macedonian access to the Peloponnesus.

In 243 B.C., a larcenous quartet of Syrian brothers living in Corinth provided Aratus with the opportunity to steal Acrocorinth's citadel from the more powerful Macedonians. Diocles, one of the brothers, was a soldier in the Macedonian garrison atop Acrocorinth. His three siblings, less respectful of lawful authority, had broken into a Macedonian treasury and stolen a substantial quantity of gold. One of these brothers, Erginus, began making occasional trips to Sicyon to fence the gold to a banker who also handled Aratus' financial transactions.

As he grew friendly with the Sicyonian banker, Erginus told him that, while making trips to visit his brother Diocles in the citadel atop Acrocorinth, he had detected a weakness in its fortifications. A side cleft, running at an angle across the face of the rock, afforded protected access to the walls at a place where they were only fifteen feet high and, thus, easily scaled by ladder. Informed of this by his banker, Aratus enlisted Erginus and Diocles in a conspiracy to seize Acrocorinth in a daring commando-type raid, promising them the immense reward of sixty talents if the enterprise was successful.

The weakness in the fortifications identified by Erginus was real enough, but there was one major complication. This vulnerable section of Acrocorinth's walls faced Corinth, rather than out to the surrounding countryside. To reach it, Aratus and his attacking force would first be required to penetrate Corinth's outer city wall, which ran from Acrocorinth down to the sea, then in darkness make their way through several miles of the city's suburbs to the bottom of the mountain. Finally, they would need to climb the steep and difficult path leading up to the cleft, while lugging weapons, shields, and fifteen-foot-long scaling ladders. They would have to accomplish all this, moreover, without alerting the city's garrison to their presence.

On the date selected for their attempt, Aratus led four hundred Achaean soldiers to the outskirts of Corinth. Erginus and seven others, disguised as travelers, went ahead to the city's western gate on the road to Sicyon. They overpowered and killed the outside sentries, but the gate remained shut. Aratus and an advance party of a hundred men scrambled up scaling ladders and over the battlements, then set off toward Acrocorinth at a run. As they moved through the darkened streets of the sleeping town, they encountered a night watch of four Macedonian guards. They killed three, but the fourth escaped to raise the alarm. Trumpets sounded, and oil lamps flared in the houses of the city and along the ramparts of Acrocorinth far above. Running soldiers filled the streets as pandemonium broke out in all quarters.

Aratus and the advance guard scrambled up Acrocorinth's steep, rocky slopes in the darkness, searching frantically for the lower end of the cleft. Providentially, the clouds parted and moonlight illuminated the terrain just long enough for them

to see how to reach the wall's vulnerable point. Then the clouds closed again, shrouding Aratus and his men in darkness during the last critical moments, as the scaling ladders were wrestled into place and the first barefooted Achaean soldiers clambered over the ramparts.

Meanwhile, the remaining three hundred men in Aratus' assault party had opened the western gate and entered the city. They could hear the sounds of fighting and the anxious blasts of trumpets from above, but the noise echoed and reverberated off the mountain's flanks in such a way that all sense of direction was lost. Desperately confused, the remaining Achaeans hid themselves in the deep shadow cast by the northern face of the mountain. They had barely taken cover when the main body of the Macedonian garrison came into view, jogging uphill from the city and shouting encouragement to their comrades in the citadel above. The Achaeans rose as if from a deliberately planned ambush and charged down on the Macedonians, scattering them in flight. Erginus then arrived from above to show them the path up the mountain, and the combined force of the Achaeans overwhelmed the citadel's garrison.

Afterward, the people of Corinth greeted Aratus with a thunderous ovation in the theater. They later erected statues of him and each of his soldiers at public expense. Plutarch hailed the capture of Acrocorinth as "the last of the Grecian exploits, being comparable to the best of them, both for the daringness of it, and the success." The bitterly disappointed Antigonus, who had lived just a little too long, died four years later at the age of eighty.

While Aratus had taught Antigonus a painful lesson about the vagaries of fortune, the Achaean League general, too, would ultimately learn that the joy of winning Acrocorinth was equaled only by the bitterness of losing it. Twenty years later, Sicyon and the other cities of the league found themselves threatened by the resurgent power of Sparta under its revolutionary king, Cleomenes III. With Sicyon itself in danger, Aratus was forced to turn to the only military power strong enough to save him from the Spartans—Macedon, now ruled by Antigonus III, the nephew and namesake of the Achaean League's former enemy.

Not surprisingly, the Macedonians demanded a high price for their support—the return of Acrocorinth. Aratus had no choice but to agree. In 222 B.C., the Macedonians fulfilled their side of the bargain by destroying the Spartan army at Sellasia. The last ten years of Aratus' life, however, were shadowed by accusations that he had betrayed the region's independence to the Macedonians. And when Antigonus III's successor, the cruel and ambitious Philip V, came to the throne, Acrocorinth, together with the other strategically located Macedonian fortresses of Chalcis and Demetrias, became collectively known as "the Fetters of Greece."

By the start of the second century B.C., the increasingly powerful Roman republic was making its influence felt from across the Adriatic. In a succession of wars between 200 and 146 B.C., Rome first displaced Macedon as the dominant power

Plutarch hailed the capture of Acrocorinth as 'the last of the Grecian exploits.'

in the Greek world, then established itself as an imperial overlord, putting a final end to the quarrelsome independence of the Greek states.

Acrocorinth witnessed both the high hopes attending the Romans' arrival as apparent liberators and the fury of destruction that marked their final conquest a bare half-century later. After Rome decisively defeated Philip V at Cynoscephalae in 197 B.C., it compelled the Macedonians to withdraw their garrisons from Acrocorinth and the other Fetters of Greece. For a time, Roman garrisons replaced them. But at a council at Corinth in 194, the philhellene Roman general Quinctius Flamininus proclaimed the freedom of the Greek states and the withdrawal of the garrisons. The Roman historian Livy described the scene that followed: "The meeting had not yet been adjourned when they caught sight of the garrison coming down from Acrocorinth, marching straightaway to the city gate, and making their departure. The general followed his troops, attended by all the delegates in a body, while they hailed him as their preserver and the liberator."

Once Macedon was conclusively defeated by the Romans in 167 B.C., however, Roman–Achaean League relations began to grow tense. In 147 B.C., Rome provoked a climactic showdown by demanding that the league detach its most important members, including Argos, Sparta, and Corinth, which would effectively deprive it of any power. The Achaeans chose to fight, but they were no match for Rome's formidable military machine. The Romans smashed them in a succession of four battles, first in central Greece and finally on the Isthmus of Corinth, a few miles from the gates of the city. Corinth's surviving garrison fled, and the Roman commander, Lucius Mummius, gave the city to his troops to burn and loot. Of the citizens who did not flee, the men were slain and the women and children sold into slavery.

Fifty years before, Corinth's citizens had cheered as the Roman legionaries voluntarily evacuated Acrocorinth. Now, in the aftermath of the Achaean

Top: Acrocorinth's first, second, and third walls (bottom to top) on the citadel's western slope are dominated by the cliffs over which Leon Sgouros leapt to his death on horseback in 1208. Above left: The most likely site of Aratus' 243 B.C. attack. Above right: The second and third walls as seen from the Frankish tower, circa 1250, in the southwest section of Acrocorinth.

War, the Romans tried to render Corinth indefensible and uninhabitable. The city's outer walls were pulled down, and efforts were also made to topple the massive fortifications atop Acrocorinth. The greatest damage was done to the double set of walls guarding the citadel's western approaches, where a steep but manageable slope descends to the low saddle connecting Acrocorinth with the adjoining height of Penteskuphi.

The Romans' destruction, however, was not complete. The Roman geographer Strabo, who visited Acrocorinth in 29 B.C., reported that when he went up the mountain "the ruins of the encircling walls were plainly visible." The archaeologists who surveyed the walls for the American School of Classical Studies at Athens in the 1920s and '30s likewise concluded that "the great wall-base defied the efforts of the soldiery who—in many stretches at least—made no effort to dislodge the two or three lowest courses of great blocks." In many places, the bottom courses of the ancient wall survive today, at some locations to nearly the height of a man.

For a century after the Roman conquest, Corinth was a ghost town, peopled only by squatters. In 44 B.C., Julius Caesar refounded the city as a Roman colony, and its unmatched location at the intersection of several trade routes soon restored it

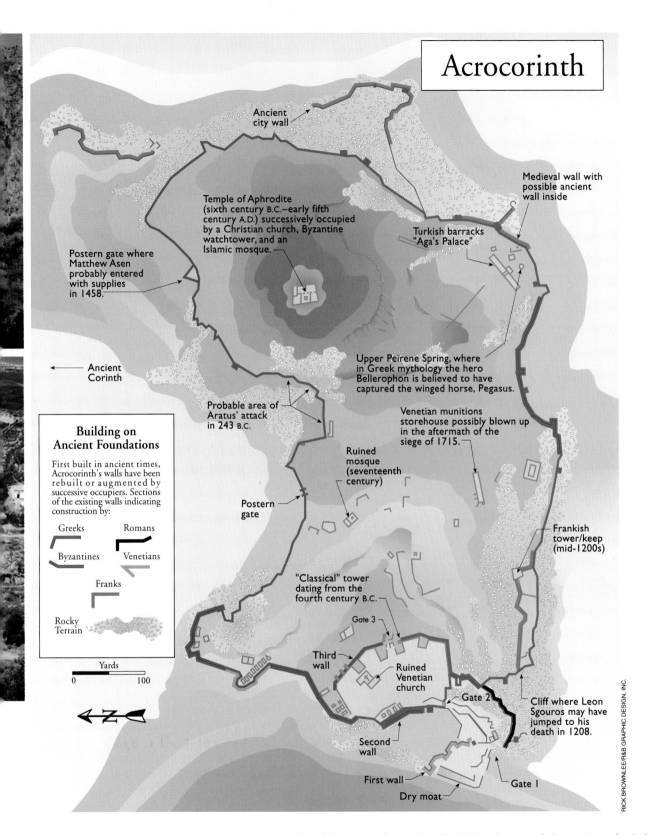

Acrocorinth

Ancient city wall

Medieval wall with possible ancient wall inside

Temple of Aphrodite (sixth century B.C.–early fifth century A.D.) successively occupied by a Christian church, Byzantine watchtower, and an Islamic mosque.

Turkish barracks "Aga's Palace"

Postern gate where Matthew Asen probably entered with supplies in 1458.

Ancient Corinth

Upper Peirene Spring, where in Greek mythology the hero Bellerophon is believed to have captured the winged horse, Pegasus.

Probable area of Aratus' attack in 243 B.C.

Venetian munitions storehouse possibly blown up in the aftermath of the siege of 1715.

Ruined mosque (seventeenth century)

Postern gate

Frankish tower/keep (mid-1200s)

"Classical" tower dating from the fourth century B.C.

Gate 3

Third wall

Ruined Venetian church

Gate 2

Cliff where Leon Sgouros may have jumped to his death in 1208.

Second wall

First wall

Dry moat

Gate 1

RICK BROWNLEE/R&B GRAPHIC DESIGN, INC.

Building on Ancient Foundations

First built in ancient times, Acrocorinth's walls have been rebuilt or augmented by successive occupiers. Sections of the existing walls indicating construction by:

Greeks   Romans

Byzantines   Venetians

Franks

Rocky Terrain

Yards
0   100

to great prosperity. Corinth remained the largest and wealthiest metropolis of Greece through the first centuries of the Christian era. The end of her prosperity came with devastating suddenness. In A.D. 395, the Visigoths, in the first of the great barbarian invasions that would ultimately destroy the Western Roman Empire, surged down the isthmus under their leader, Alaric, to overwhelm Corinth's defenders. The resulting sack and slaughter exceeded that of Mummius, five hundred years

earlier. When the Visigoths moved deeper into the Peloponnesus, they left behind smoking ruins and mass graves. The Dark Ages had come to Corinth.

There followed a thousand years of danger and instability, during which the city sometimes shrank to a beleaguered settlement sheltering within Acrocorinth's protective walls. In the middle third of the sixth century, when Justinian ruled the Eastern Roman, or Byzantine, Empire, Acrocorinth's walls

The imposing citadel of Acrocorinth can be seen in the background of these ancient Roman ruins known as the "West Shops" near the present-day museum at the foot of the mountain.

were rebuilt, and a huge cistern with massive brick vaults was constructed that survives today. In the twelfth century, the city grew wealthy from its silk factories. Unfortunately, its prosperity attracted the attention of Norman freebooters from the kingdom of Sicily, who took and sacked both the lower city and Acrocorinth during a raid in 1147.

The longest of Acrocorinth's many sieges came at the beginning of the thirteenth century. In 1204, the misguided warriors of the Fourth Crusade captured Constantinople, which they considered the capital of a schismatic church, barely less dangerous to Catholic Christendom than Islam. With the fall of Constantinople, the Byzantine Empire shattered into fragments. Both the ambitious, land-hungry Crusaders—most of whom were Franks, or Frenchmen—and various Byzantine provincial leaders scrambled to pick up the pieces and create new principalities for themselves. The fortress atop Acrocorinth was one of the most important prizes in play.

Byzantine resistance to the Frankish invaders on mainland Greece was led by the archon of Nauplia, Leon Sgouros. Sgouros was a representative figure of those insecure times—ambitious and unscrupulous, physically brave and savagely cruel. He made himself master of Corinth just before the fall of Constantinople to the Franks. When the Metropolitan Nicholas, archbishop of the city, denounced the rapacity of his troops and tax collectors, Sgouros invited him to dinner one evening in the citadel—where his troops seized the unfortunate prelate, blinded him, and hurled him from Acrocorinth's cliffs to his death.

After Constantinople fell, Sgouros awaited the coming of the Franks "holed up in Acrocorinth like a shaggy beast, or a creeping serpent coiled up in its lair," according to the contemporary Byzantine historian Nicetas Choniates. In the spring of 1205, the Frankish army arrived, captured the lower town, and laid siege to the citadel. Although Sgouros had little hope of relief, he conducted the defense with courage and imagination. The French chronicler Geoffrey de Villehardouin wrote that Sgouros, "a very shrewd and wily man," noticed that the Frankish commander, Jacques d'Avesnes, "had only a small body of men with him, and did not keep good watch. So one morning at daybreak he came out of the city in full force, and got as far as the tents and killed many of our men before they could lay hold of their arms." D'Avesnes himself was wounded in this sortie.

After that setback, the Franks tightened the siege. Among other works, they erected a small castle atop the conical hill of Penteskuphi, some four thousand feet southwest of Acrocorinth. It still survives today, plainly visible to the right of the road leading up the mountain.

Despite these efforts, the siege dragged on for five years. Siegecraft was poorly developed in medieval times, and a vigorously defended fortress could usually withstand an attacker until either thirst or hunger forced its garrison to submit. Water was

not a problem because of the multitude of springs within Acrocorinth's walls, but the citadel's great stores of food would eventually be depleted. Boredom and claustrophobia could also work to undermine the defenders' morale.

Sgouros' sanity ultimately broke under these pressures. In the third year of the siege, overwhelmed by despair and "unable to bear the state of slavery," according to a later chronicler, he took his own life in an unforgettable manner. Choosing a place near the edge of a steep cliff—most likely that along the southwest side of the citadel—he spurred his horse over the wall in a suicidal leap. Horse and rider plunged dramatically into the void before smashing on the rocks far below, where Sgouros' body was so badly mangled that "not even one of his bones remained unshattered," according to a medieval author. Sgouros' final fall curiously echoed his own murder of the Metropolitan Nicholas five years earlier.

But even the bizarre death of their commander did not break the Greek garrison's will to resist. Michael Angelus, a prince who had established his own principality in the northwestern Greek territory of Epirus, sent a force south under his halfbrother, Theodore. Theodore broke through the siege lines around Acrocorinth, reinforcing the garrison and replenishing its food supply, and took command of the citadel's defense. The siege continued for two more years. Eventually, in April 1210, Geoffrey de Villehardouin, a Frankish knight (and a nephew of the chronicler) who had established his rule throughout most of the Peloponnesus, assumed command of the besiegers. Geoffrey tightened his grip around the fortress until the garrison was compelled in autumn to ask for terms.

Acrocorinth experienced a varied succession of Frankish and Italian rulers over the next two centuries before eventually returning to Byzantine rule in 1395. By then, however, time was running out for the surviving fragments of Byzantium, now reduced to a tribute-paying vassal of the Ottoman Turks. In May 1453, the Turks cut the heart out of the dying empire when they conquered Constantinople and killed Constantine XI, the last Byzantine emperor.

Corinth and the rest of the Peloponnesus clung to independence for a few more years under the rule of Demetrius and Thomas Palaeologus, the quarrelsome younger brothers of the dead Constantine. But they lacked the military resources, diplomatic allies, and political sagacity that would have been necessary to maintain their precarious position on the outer edge of the expanding Ottoman Empire. By the spring of 1458, Demetrius and Thomas were three years behind on the annual tribute of twelve thousand gold ducats they owed to Mehmet II, the ruthless and ambitious young Ottoman sultan. Mehmet decided to teach them a lesson, and on May 15, 1458, he led a great army into the Peloponnesus. Corinth was his first target.

Corinth's governor, Matthew Asen, who came from a distinguished family of Greco-Bulgarian nobility, was a courageous and resourceful leader. He was at Nauplia when the sultan's invasion began, but his deputy organized a spirited defense, and the garrison and townspeople drove off the initial Turkish attacks. Several nights later, Asen and seventy men set out from the Corinthian port at Cenchrae, laboring under the weight of extra weapons and bags of corn. They successfully evaded the Turkish sentries under cover of darkness and slipped through the siege lines into the fortress. (They probably scaled the eastern side of the mountain below the upper peak and were admitted by the garrison through a postern gate—later bricked up by the Turks—into a triangular bastion that juts out from the northeast wall of the fortress.)

Once he arrived, Asen conducted such a vigorous defense that Mehmet decided to leave part of his army behind under the grand vizier to continue the siege. The sultan then marched south to ravage other parts of the peninsula.

Two months later, Mehmet returned to find Asen and the garrison of Acrocorinth still holding out. For a fortnight, Mehmet battered the citadel's ancient walls with his huge cannons, which could hurl stone balls weighing almost nine hundred pounds a mile and half. Eventually, the pounding opened a breach in the outer wall, and Mehmet ordered an assault on Acrocorinth's western approaches. After a desperate hand-to-hand struggle, the Turkish janissaries broke through the outer line of the defenses and poured into the area between the first and second walls. Here, however, they were overwhelmed by a hail of missiles from both the second wall and the fortifications below the lower peak, forcing them to retire with heavy losses.

The defenders' victory was short-lived. Mehmet resumed the bombardment with his great artillery. The bakehouse and the magazines inside the fortress were destroyed, and the concentrated pounding eventually smashed the second gate and its adjoining tower. Inside the fortress, all knew there was no hope of relief. The metropolitan of Corinth, fearful of the consequences if the town were taken by assault, opened secret negotiations with the sultan. When Asen realized that the majority inside the citadel were opposed to further resistance, he agreed to terms, and the fortress surrendered on August 6.

Mehmet treated his defeated enemies with respect. He allowed Asen and his exhausted garrison to march out with the honors of war, while the city's inhabitants were ordered to pay tribute but were otherwise left unmolested. A Turkish bey was installed as governor of Acrocorinth, along with a garrison of four hundred men picked from Mehmet's own bodyguard—the same number that Aratus had designated to defend the fortress seventeen hundred years earlier.

When the Greeks revolted against the Turks in the 1820s, sympathetic western European audiences proved eager for accounts of earlier struggles between outnumbered Greeks and the limitless forces of the Ottoman sultan. One prominent philhellene was the young Italian Romantic composer Gioacchino

Rossini, the artistic director of the Paris Opera. In October 1825, his first French opera, *The Siege of Corinth*, opened to a rapturous public response.

Rossini's opera took the siege of 1458 as its starting point, but its treatment bore little resemblance to the actual events. In place of the impoverished community huddled within the walls of Acrocorinth that Matthew Asen actually governed, Rossini's opera is set against such backdrops as "the Governor's Palace" or "the vestibule of the Palace of the Senate in Corinth." The opera tells the story of Pamira, daughter of the Greek governor Cleomene, who is torn between her father's desire to see her engaged to a young Greek officer named Neocle and her own love for a mysterious Turk she knows as Almanzor, but who is ultimately revealed to be Sultan Mehmet II himself. Mehmet offers to spare the city if she will marry him. But Pamira ultimately chooses duty and country over love. In the last scene, as the defenders are overwhelmed and the Turks break into the city, Pamira kills herself rather than fall into Mehmet's hands, while Corinth burns in the background. *The Siege of Corinth* was a major success for Rossini and continues to enjoy regular performances today.

Once the Turks established their rule over most of Greece in 1461, Acrocorinth lost most of its importance. It was only when the long decline of Ottoman power began in the late seventeenth century that Acrocorinth again resumed a significant military role. In 1687, the Venetians reclaimed the Peloponnesus from the Turks, who were in disarray following the failure of their final great siege of Vienna four years earlier. The Venetians extensively reconditioned Acrocorinth's aging fortress, but these efforts did little good when a Turkish army of one hundred thousand men marched against it in the summer of 1715. This episode inspired one of Lord Byron's finest narrative poems, *The Siege of Corinth*, published in January 1816. But Byron had to take a great deal of dramatic license, because the real event was glorious for neither side. The Venetian and Greek garrison of six hundred men resisted the overwhelming Turkish force for only a few days before surrendering. And in a foreshadowing of other Balkan tragedies to come, most of the garrison was massacred or sold into slavery after they surrendered their weapons. A century later, when the fortress fell to insurgents in 1822 during the Greek War of Independence, most of the Turkish captives suffered a similar fate.

Greek soldiers continued to be posted atop Acrocorinth for a few years after the country had won its independence from the Turks in 1827. But the frontier of the new Greek kingdom ran well to the north of Corinth. Given its diminished strategic significance, there was no point in reconditioning Acrocorinth's long-neglected fortifications. After two and a half millennia of military service, dating back to the time of Cypselids, Acrocorinth was a fortress no longer.

JEFFERSON M. GRAY writes from Reisterstown, Maryland. This is his first *MHQ* contribution.

> For a fortnight, Mehmet battered the citadel's ancient walls with his huge cannons.

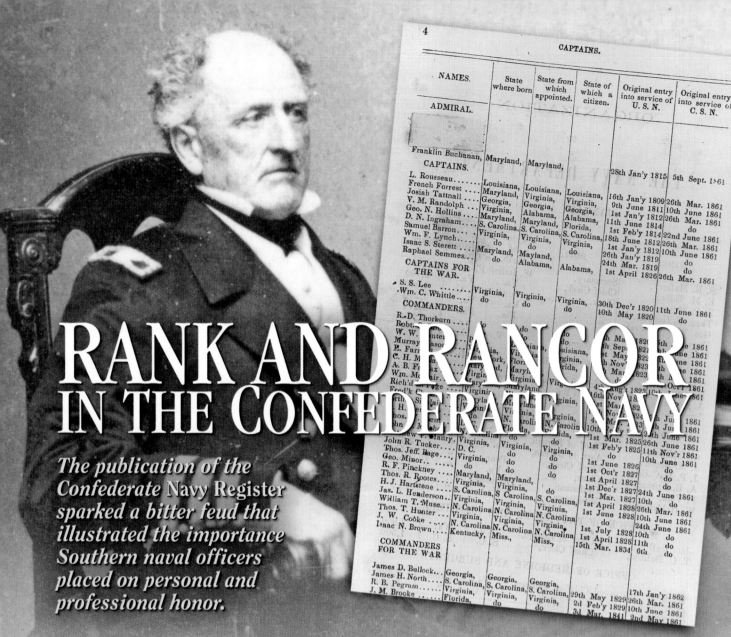

NAMES.	State where born.	State from which appointed.	State of which a citizen.	Original entry into service of U. S. N.	Original entry into service of C. S. N.
ADMIRAL.					
Franklin Buchanan,	Maryland,	Maryland,		28th Jan'y 1815	5th Sept. 1861
CAPTAINS.					
L. Rousseau......	Louisiana,	Louisiana,	Louisiana,	16th Jan'y 1809	26th Mar. 1861
French Forrest	Maryland,	Virginia,	Virginia,	9th June 1811	10th June 1861
Josiah Tattnall	Georgia,	Georgia,	Georgia,	1st Jan'y 1812	26th Mar. 1861
V. M. Randolph ...	Virginia,	Alabama,	Alabama,	11th June 1814	do
Geo. N. Hollins ...	Maryland,	Maryland,	Florida,	1st Feb'y 1814	22nd June 1861
D. N. Ingraham ...	S. Carolina,	S. Carolina,	S. Carolina,	18th June 1812	26th Mar. 1861
Samuel Barron...	Virginia,	Virginia,	Virginia,	1st Jan'y 1812	10th June 1861
Wm. F. Lynch ...	do	do	do	26th Jan'y 1819	do
Isaac S. Sterett	Maryland,	Mayland,		24th Mar. 1819	do
Raphael Semmes...	do	Alabama,	Alabama,	1st April 1826	26th Mar. 1861
CAPTAINS FOR THE WAR.					
S. S. Lee	Virginia,	Virginia,	Virginia,	30th Dec'r 1820	11th June 1861
Wm. C. Whittle	do	do	do	10th May 1820	do
COMMANDERS.					
R. D. Thorburn ...		do	do		
Robt.			do		
W. W. ...	inter...		do		
Murray ...sor...	...nia,	...nial...		...th Ma...	...e 1861
E. Farr...		New York,	...uisiana,	...st Ma...	...e 1861
C. H. M...	...nia,	Florid...	...rginia,	...t Nov...	...e 1861
A. B. Fa...ix	...Mar...	Maryl...	...rida,	...823	...e 1861
Wm. Mc...lin	...Virgin...	Mary...	...rginia,	...Mar...	...e 1861
Rich'd ...rge	...ary...nd	...arylan...	Vir...	4..Aug't 1823	Oct'r 1861
Fred'k ...t...	...rth Si...	...yla...	...rginia.	...Nov..18...	...861
H.	...nd	...N....	...rt Mar...	...861	
Thos.	...nia	...N...	...rolina,	...e 1861	
...hn	...nd	...Flori...	...da,	10th ...r...	...Ju... 1861
...lew ...Maury.	Virginia,		do	...t Mar. 1825	...Ju... 1861
John R. Tucker ...	Virginia,	Virginia,	do	1st Feb'y 1825	26th June 1861
Thos. Jeff. Page...	D. C.	do	Virginia,	do	11th Nov'r 1861
Geo. Minor...	Virginia,	do	do	1st June 1826	10th June 1861
R. F. Pinckney ...	do	Maryland,	do	1st Oct'r 1827	do
Thos. R. Rootes...	Maryland,	Virginia,	do	1st April 1827	do
H. J. Hartstene ...	Virginia,	S Carolina,	S. Carolina,	1st Dec'r 1827	do
Jas. L. Henderson..	S. Carolina,	Virginia,	Virginia,	1st Mar. 1827	24th June 1861
William T. Muse...	Virginia,	N. Carolina,	do	1st April 1828	10th Mar. 1861
Thos. T. Hunter ...	N. Carolina,	Virginia,	Virginia,	1st June 1828	26th Mar. 1861
J. W. Cooke ...	Virginia,	N. Carolina,	N. Carolina,	do	10th June 1861
Isaac N. Brown ...	N. Carolina,	N. Carolina,	N. Carolina,	1st July 1828	24th June 1861
	Kentucky,	Miss.,	Miss.,	1st April 1828	10th do
COMMANDERS FOR THE WAR				15th Mar. 1834	11th do
					6th do
James D. Bullock...	Georgia,	Georgia,	Georgia,		17th Jan'y 1862
James H. North	S. Carolina,	S. Carolina,	S. Carolina,	29th May 1829	26th Mar. 1861
R. B. Pegram	Virginia,	Virginia,	Virginia,	2d Feb'y 1829	10th June 1861
J. M. Brooke	Florida,	do	do	3d Mar. 1841	2nd May 1861

RANK AND RANCOR IN THE CONFEDERATE NAVY

The publication of the Confederate Navy Register sparked a bitter feud that illustrated the importance Southern naval officers placed on personal and professional honor.

by Craig L. Symonds

The first official list of United States Navy officers appeared in 1800, when the navy itself was only a half-dozen years old. A slim pamphlet, only twelve pages long, it was nevertheless much in demand by the twenty-six captains, nine masters commandant, and 108 lieutenants whose names, ranks, and dates of commission it listed. This little booklet, after all, allowed officers to survey the names of those who were ahead of them on the ladder of seniority and to calculate their own chances for preferment or promotion.

Fifteen years later, at the close of the War of 1812, the Navy Department began publication of an annual listing of officers in what became known as *The Naval Register*. From that date forward, the volume could be found in the papers of virtually every serving officer. The *Register* told them how many officers there were at each rank and where they were serving. In addition, it indicated who was senior to whom within each grade, important information since even a few days' seniority could be decisive. For example, a captain who was only a week senior to another would be entitled to act as commodore if the two ever operated together in a squadron. Emblematic of an orderly profession where relative status was clearly defined, *The Navy Register* also represented a kind of public validation of each officer's professional worth and accomplishments.

When the Civil War broke out in 1861, the Confederate navy adopted many of the traditions of the United States Navy, including the publication of an annual *Navy Register*. The December 1862 *Register* was the first full-scale Confederate effort to produce such a public record. Thirty-eight pages long, it listed all 473 Confederate navy officers (including midshipmen) by date of rank and also included an officer's pay table and even the laws of the navy. But that *Register* also provoked a bitter quarrel between two of the service's most senior officers—Flag Officer French Forrest, chief of the Bureau of Orders and Detail, and Admiral Franklin Buchanan, commander of the Mobile Bay Squadron. Their feud provides a window into the personalities of two of the Confederacy's senior officers, as well as the whole issue of personal and professional honor in the value system of the Confederate navy.

The seeds of the quarrel may well have been planted a decade earlier, when the two men were on opposite sides of a public debate about how to reform the promotion system in the United States Navy. As a member of a so-called Efficiency Board in 1855, then-Commander Buchanan had voted to compel the retirement from active service of scores of officers whom he found to be either too old or insufficiently meritorious. Although Forrest was not one of those forced to retire, he objected to the whole proceeding as injurious to good order and discipline. In the intervening years, neither man modified his view. Buchanan continued to espouse a promotion system that allowed active and deserving junior officers to jump past their elderly seniors, and Forrest continued to insist on retaining the time-proven method of advancement by seniority.

When the Confederate navy was established in 1861, Southern lawmakers adopted a policy that accommodated both views. In fact, the creation of an entirely new army and navy allowed the Confederacy to rethink a rank structure that was, in large part, the result of traditions dating back to the British experience. For example, the U.S. Congress had never seen fit to establish a military rank above that of major general in the army, or captain in the navy. This decision derived, in part, from a republican reluctance to elevate officers to a public status that might enable them to pose a threat to civilian government and the rule of law. Then, too, because George Washington had held the rank of three-star general, most legislators believed it unfitting for any other officer to hold an equivalent rank. Winfield Scott boasted a brevet

Admiral Franklin Buchanan (opposite left) accused Captain French Forrest (right) of minimizing Buchanan's accomplishments and status by including four dotted lines above his name in the Confederate Navy Register. *Inset left: The dotted lines were later covered with a paper patch (Opposite left and Right: U.S. Naval Historical Center; Inset: Courtesy of Craig L. Symonds).*

rank as a three-star general after the Mexican War, but neither he nor anyone else had ever held a statutory rank of lieutenant general. Not until 1864 did Congress abandon this tradition, in order to bestow the rank of lieutenant general on Ulysses S. Grant.

As for the navy, the early Congress had even more serious concerns. In part, these derived from British tradition. Ever since the English Civil Wars in the seventeenth century, the ground troops in England (remodeled by Oliver Cromwell in the service of Parliament) had been called the British army, while the sea service (which had stood by the Crown) had been called the Royal Navy. In much the same spirit, most congressmen tended to view the American army as a kind of expanded militia—that is, as an extension of America itself—whereas navies, with their traditions of aristocracy, were perceived as tools of empire. Consequently, Congress had deliberately avoided establishing the rank of admiral in the U.S. Navy at all, in the belief that admirals and democracies were incompatible.

The Confederate founding fathers suffered no such scruples. Despite a reverence for George Washington (whose image appeared on the official Confederate seal), they created ranks of both lieutenant general (three stars) and even general (four stars) for the Confederate army. And they established the ranks of both rear admiral and admiral for the Confederate navy, though the legislation also decreed that there could be only four admirals. Significantly, however, the law also decreed that the rank of admiral would not go to the most senior officers but must be reserved exclusively for those who earned the distinction by "gallant and meritorious conduct" in battle. In part, this was a protection against the emergence of "political admirals," but in the main, it was a reflection of the Southern value system, in which great

deeds in battle, more than successful bureaucratic maneuvering or mere seniority, would characterize and distinguish the true heroes of the new nation.

The principal beneficiary of this legislation was Captain Franklin Buchanan. "Old Buck" was sixty-one when the Civil War broke out. A forty-five-year veteran of the United States Navy, he had joined as a midshipman in the waning days of the War of 1812 and had a long and distinguished career of service. He had been the founding superintendent of the United States Naval Academy at Annapolis, commanded a warship in the war with Mexico, and captained Matthew Perry's flagship during that officer's famous voyage to

are all with the South," he hesitated to commit himself to the Confederacy. Not until midsummer, after Confederate land forces had fought and won the First Battle of Manassas, did he bid farewell to his family and his home on Maryland's Eastern Shore and cross the Potomac to offer his services to the Confederate navy.

Confederate naval legislation aided Buchanan in two ways. First, he benefited from the law that declared that any U.S. Navy officer who resigned his commission to come south and fight for the Confederacy was entitled to an equal rank in the infant Confederate navy. Thus, Buchanan entered the C.S. Navy as a captain. Second, the provision that

That appointment was a huge disappointment for French Forrest, who, as commandant of the Gosport Navy Yard at Norfolk, had spent much of the winter presiding over the phoenix-like rebirth of *Virginia* from the charred hull of the old wooden frigate *Merrimack*. Like Buchanan, Forrest was a Marylander by birth, with a distinguished career in the U.S. Navy. When he and Buchanan had each resigned in April 1861, Forrest had immediately pledged himself to Virginia and the Confederacy, while Buchanan had waited five months before making a similar decision. Both men were personally brave. Captain William H. Parker wrote that Forrest "did not know the meaning of the word 'fear.'" But Forrest seldom acted without lengthy deliberation, and Mallory did not believe that he had the necessary aggressive instinct to command *Virginia*. The Confederate navy secretary therefore deliberately passed over Forrest in selecting Buchanan for the command.

As the captain of Virginia, *Buchanan won fame and a promotion to admiral when his ironclad destroyed the wooden warships* Cumberland *(above) and* Congress *on March 8, 1862, in Hampton Roads, Virginia. The sixty-one-year-old officer was wounded during the fight, however, and missed* Virginia's *subsequent duel with the Union ironclad* Monitor.

"open" Japan to the West in 1853. When the Civil War erupted in 1861, he was the commandant of the Washington Navy Yard. Because he was a Marylander and a slave owner, Buchanan's views on the sectional conflict were somewhat ambivalent. He continued to do his duty, declaring that the navy yard would be defended against "any person or persons…to the last extremity." But news of the so-called Pratt Street Massacre in Baltimore led him to conclude that in such a crisis "every Marylander should be at his post," and he resigned his commission on April 22. Even though he declared that his "heart, feelings, and sympathies

promotions to the rank of admiral had to be earned by "gallant and meritorious service" suited him just fine. It was a policy he had long advocated, and he was sufficiently confident of his own abilities to believe that if fate gave him the opportunity, he would be able to make the most of it. And sure enough, fate, in the person of Confederate navy Secretary Stephen Mallory, did give him the opportunity. After a brief stint in Richmond as chief of the Bureau of Orders and Detail, Mallory appointed Buchanan to command the James River Squadron with the brand-new (and as yet untested) ironclad *Virginia* as his flagship.

Forrest was reduced to the status of a witness when on March 8, 1862, Buchanan conned the ironclad *Virginia* out into Hampton Roads and made history by destroying two Federal warships—*Congress* and *Cumberland*—each more heavily armed than his own ship, thereby demonstrating the superiority of armored warships over traditional wooden vessels. Wounded at the very moment of victory, Buchanan was unable to participate in the next day's historic confrontation of CSS *Virginia* against USS *Monitor*, but the Confederate Congress was nevertheless rapturous about the victory he had achieved over the two wooden Federal warships. Mallory's report declared, "The dashing courage and consummate professional ability of Flag Officer Buchanan and his associates achieved the most remarkable victory which naval annals record." Josiah Tattnall, who succeeded Buchanan to the command of the James River Squadron, said that simple justice would compel Congress to "make [him] an admiral and put [him] at the head of [their] navy."

These encomiums were not entirely undeserved. Buchanan had demonstrated both aggressiveness and determination. But the euphoria that pervaded Confederate Richmond in the aftermath of the battle derived, in part, from the nearly universal belief that the Confederate navy had unveiled a superweapon that could reverse the course of the war. The drawn battle between *Virginia* and the little *Monitor* on March 9 did nothing to mute the enthusiasm for Buchanan's achievement, for it was less evident at the time than in hindsight that the arrival of *Monitor* had effectively neutralized the offensive potential of *Virginia*.

Not everyone was euphoric. Forrest believed that Buchanan was merely the beneficiary of a technological breakthrough. He asserted that any officer in command of such a craft could have destroyed two wooden ships lying at anchor. Forrest believed that he almost certainly could have done it himself—and indeed would have if Mallory had followed custom and bestowed the honor of command upon the senior officer present.

And Forrest's pique welled into a full-scale funk when he learned that in conformance with the Confederate naval policy, Mallory planned to recommend Buchanan for a promotion to the rank of admiral for "gallant and meritorious service." Congress enthusiastically accepted the recommendation, and Buchanan became the Confederacy's first and, as it would turn out, only, full admiral. The news almost made Forrest physically sick. Navy Lieutenant John Taylor Wood reported to his friend Catesby Jones, *Virginia*'s executive officer, that "Admiral Buchanan's promotion laid Commodore Forrest up for some days. He was not visible at the office." When Forrest at last emerged, he did so in order to conspire with several other senior officers (George T. Sinclair, Ebenezer Farrand, and Robert Pegam, among others) to repeal the legislation declaring that promotions to admiral must come as the result of "conspicuous gallantry." According to the disapproving Wood, Forrest much preferred the old system of promotion by seniority.

Forrest's attempt to repeal the offending legislation never got off the ground, and in the days after the fight in Hampton Roads, he did little to work his way into Mallory's good graces. Two weeks after *Virginia* withdrew from her clash with *Monitor* back into the navy yard at Norfolk, Mallory wrote Forrest to ask why the repairs on the ironclad were

Confederate navy Secretary Stephen R. Mallory grew frustrated with Forrest, commandant of the Norfolk navy yard, because of the slow pace of repairs to Virginia, *and reassigned him.*

taking so long. The navy secretary's impatience was evident: "The work of getting the *Virginia*…ready for sea at the earliest possible moment is the most important duty that could devolve upon a naval officer at this time," he wrote, "and yet…I am not advised that a day's work has been done upon the *Virginia* since she went into dock." Three days later, Mallory followed up this letter with a terse telegram: "Report the condition of your vessel. Is she ready for service? If not, when will she be?" Forrest might have been surprised to see Mallory refer to *Virginia* as "your vessel," for he still did not have command. That had gone to Josiah Tattnall. Apparently, however, Mallory still held Forrest responsible for the slow progress of the repairs, for the very next day he removed him from his duties as navy yard commander, sending Captain Smith Lee, Robert E. Lee's brother, to take charge of the yard. Forrest got a desk job in Richmond as the chief of the Bureau of Orders and Detail, the position that Buchanan had held when he first arrived in Richmond the previous September.

As for Buchanan, he was still recovering from his injuries in a Norfolk hospital, and the news of his elevation to admiral was especially gratifying. He praised his officers and crew and thanked Mallory for the honor, but had to do so through an amanuensis since he could not raise

himself from his bed to write. In fact, he remained out of action for five months. When in August he finally reported himself ready for duty, Mallory sent him to take command of the small Confederate squadron in Mobile Bay.

Buchanan was trying to patch together the naval defenses there when he received his copy of the *Register of the Commissioned and Warrant Officers of the Navy of the Confederate States to January 1, 1863*. For the first time ever, a navy register began not with a listing of "Captains," but with the heading "Admiral"—expressed in the singular since there was only one. And sure enough, there was his name, Franklin Buchanan, listed under that heading. But above his name were four dotted lines—evident place holders—as if to suggest that the four admirals senior to Buchanan were still pending or simply had not yet been identified.

Perplexed by this curious entry, Buchanan queried Mallory. "As I am not aware that there are four admirals above me in the Navy," he wrote, "I respectfully ask an explanation of the dotted lines." Mallory replied that the compilation of the *Register* was the responsibility of the Bureau of Orders and Detail—that is, the responsibility of French Forrest.

No record exists to prove that Forrest intended the four dotted lines to appear in print. The lines may simply have been intended as place holders while the publication was being designed. If that were the case, however, why was the heading the singular "Admiral," rather than the plural "Admirals"? Perhaps Forrest included the dotted lines to signify that not all four of the admirals authorized by law had yet been identified. If so, why insert four lines rather than three—Buchanan had already been appointed—and why place those lines above, rather than below, Buchanan's name? Perhaps the dotted lines were no more than a printer's error, or perhaps Forrest meant to imply what he certainly felt: Buchanan's promotion as admiral was some kind of a historical accident.

In any case, the news that it was Forrest who was responsible for the four dotted lines infuriated Buchanan. Forrest, he decided, was simply jealous—jealous because Buchanan had gotten command of *Virginia*, jealous because *Virginia* had won a great victory, and jealous because Buchanan had received a promotion that Forrest had wanted for himself. Forrest had always opposed the idea of promotion by merit, and having failed to prevent the adoption of such a policy, he now sought to undermine it by minimizing Buchanan's position in the navy. Buchanan believed that Forrest was attempting to imply that Buchanan was the least of admirals and sure to be surpassed in "conspicuous gallantry" by others. In Buchanan's view, such a public imputation was not only wicked but also cowardly and underhanded. Rather than confront Buchanan personally, he sought to discredit him anonymously through an official publication. Such a public aspersion was simply not to be tolerated.

Always one to shoot from the hip, Buchanan immediately sat down to write to Forrest. He declared that he was not surprised by Forrest's *little act* (italics in original) since he knew that Forrest had been disappointed not to be made an admiral. "But why you should have expected it, none of your brother officers can tell," he wrote, "for certainly you have never given any evidence, by applying for orders where there was a prospect of danger, that you wished to serve your country, or to display gallantry to secure your promotion."

This was a stunning charge, for it was effectively an accusation of cowardice, a charge that no Southern officer could allow to pass unchallenged. Forrest, Buchanan asserted, sought safe desk jobs, while he sent others to face the heat of battle. "I am aware that you have permitted seven of your Juniors to command squadrons when there was a prospect of danger without any dissatisfaction on your part, or application from you for such service." He ended with a final, devastating gibe: "Your little act, in the arrangement of the dotted lines, cannot injure me, or interfere with my position in the Navy, nor can they make you an admiral."

Buchanan's accusation was not entirely fair. While it was undoubtedly true that Forrest was jealous of Buchanan's good fortune in being tapped for command of *Virginia*, and while Buchanan's promotion had been a tremendous blow, the charge that Forrest had avoided active duty was groundless. Forrest had ea-

gerly and repeatedly sought active service at sea. It was Mallory, who distrusted both Forrest's health and his aggressiveness, who had prevented it.

Forrest might have demanded satisfaction from Buchanan for penning such a letter, but instead he sought to soothe him. Though he did not explain how or why the four dotted lines came to be in the *Navy Register* above Buchanan's name, he insisted rather vaguely that the whole matter was a misunderstanding. As for Buchanan's declaration that Forrest was a coward for avoiding active duty, Forrest reiterated that he had requested active service, but so far it had been denied to him. He wanted to serve his country and was eager for active service at sea, but Mallory had seen fit to keep him in administrative positions.

Buchanan was both skeptical and unforgiving. Despite the apologetic tone of Forrest's letter, Buchanan responded with more scorn: "I am more satisfied than ever," he replied, "of your little act in reference to the dotted lines."

That was not the end of it. A few weeks after Buchanan's last letter to Forrest, one of Buchanan's officers showed him a recent copy of the *Richmond Examiner* that contained a front-page article titled "A Strange Record." The key element of this article was the text of a letter that Buchanan had written to U.S. Secretary of the Navy Gideon Welles back in May of 1861—two years earlier. When Maryland had failed to secede from the Union as Buchanan had expected, Old Buck had attempted to withdraw his resignation. Someone had found a copy of the letter in which Buchanan had made his request and given it to the editor of Richmond's leading newspaper. It was damaging stuff. The news that Buchanan had tried to recant his resignation was bad enough, but the last line of that letter cast Buchanan in a very bad light, indeed. "I am ready for service," he had written to Welles. "Service against whom?" a Southern reader might well have asked. Had Buchanan been ready to accept orders to fight against the South? Although the newspaper let the offending letter speak for itself without editorial comment, the implication that Buchanan was less than a full Southern patriot was clear enough,

and Buchanan believed he could not let it rest without a response.

In an open letter to the editor of the *Examiner*, published two weeks later, Buchanan admitted that he had written the letter to Welles, but claimed that at the time he wrote it, it had seemed to him that "the troubles and difficulties in the country would certainly be arranged when Congress met." Based on that assumption, he had asked to recall his resignation. "This, I soon regretted," he wrote, "when it became apparent to all that there could be no reconciliation." Since then, he claimed, "My acts in the Confederacy speak for themselves."

Buchanan avoided any serious public damage from the revelation of this information, in part because of the timing of the incident. The exposé appeared on May 5, 1863, two days after Lee's astonishing and improbable victory at Chancellorsville, and five days before Thomas J. "Stonewall" Jackson's death—events that drove most other issues out of the public mind. Privately, however, Buchanan remained furious, and he directed his fury primarily at the man he was sure had leaked the letter to the press. There is no evidence that Forrest was indeed the culprit, but Buchanan needed no evidence. He believed that Forrest was too cowardly to face the enemy in battle, or even to face his accuser on the field of honor, but that he was fully capable of trying to strike back in this typically craven and backstairs way. To a friend in Richmond, Buchanan wrote that Forrest was "mean enough to do any thing."

Only days later, Buchanan heard the satisfying news that Forrest was no longer the head of the Bureau of Orders and Detail. Perhaps provoked by Buchanan's gibes, Forrest had renewed his request for an active command, and Mallory had finally gratified him by making him commodore of the James River Squadron, the same assignment Buchanan had held when he had won his promotion to admiral. By now, of course, there was little glory to be had in such an assignment. The flagship of the squadron, the ironclad *Virginia*, was gone, blown up by her own crew the year before during the Confederate evacuation of Norfolk. Forrest, therefore, presided over a squadron that existed mostly in name only, and he spent most of his time in Richmond working

While Forrest never saw action in a significant Civil War naval engagement, Buchanan again commanded an ironclad in an historic fight. During the furious Battle of Mobile Bay (above), Admiral David G. Farragut's fleet pummeled CSS Tennessee, *eventually forcing Buchanan to surrender.*

on administrative details rather than at sea engaging the enemy. Meanwhile, his place as head of the Bureau of Orders and Detail was filled by Buchanan's friend, Captain John K. Mitchell. "I am glad to see you at the head of the bureau," Buchanan wrote Mitchell when he heard the news. "We have wanted for some time a man of method and system there. Old Forrest, with his selfishness, would have ruined the Navy had he been continued there much longer."

Mitchell's presence at the head of the bureau gave Buchanan a chance to correct what he considered to be a standing insult—the removal of those offensive "four dotted lines" in the *Navy Register*. Mitchell agreed to issue a new version of the *Register*. Bearing the same date as the original, this one was only fourteen pages long, instead of thirty-eight pages. It omitted the pay table and the laws of the navy, but all 473 officers listed in the first edition appeared in the second, without a single change save one—no dotted lines above Buchanan's name. Almost certainly, the Confederate government agreed to publish an entirely new edition of the *Register* solely to soothe Buchanan's ruffled feathers.

Nor was that all. Although no letters survive to show where the idea originated, someone—either Buchanan, Mitchell, or perhaps Mallory himself—declared that existing copies of the original *Register* should be modified as well. As a result, most surviving copies of the thirty-eight-

page version of the December 1862 Confederate *Navy Register* bear a small patch on page four—a piece of paper that is glued on the page above the name of Franklin Buchanan to cover the four dotted lines that the Confederate navy's only admiral found so offensive.

As for Forrest, he never found an opportunity for glory in his brief active service in command of the little James River Squadron. Mallory replaced him in the spring of 1864, again choosing Buchanan's friend Mitchell as his successor. For his part, Buchanan soon found himself back at the vortex of naval history when he confronted Rear Admiral David G. Farragut's squadron in the Battle of Mobile Bay in August of 1864. After Farragut steamed into the bay, Buchanan attacked the entire Federal squadron with his single ironclad, CSS *Tennessee*, and carried on an unequal fight that lasted for several hours. Seriously wounded during the battle, he authorized his flag captain to raise the white flag only when *Tennessee* was no longer maneuverable or capable of defending itself. He was taken prisoner and sent to Fort Lafayette in New York Harbor, where he slowly recovered his health. He was exchanged in April 1865, just in time to be taken prisoner again at the end of the war. Forrest barely survived the war and died in 1866, largely ignored by peers and posterity alike.

Historians generally acknowledge the critical role of honor in explaining and

understanding the value system of the South. Not only was honor an issue in provoking the *Navy Register* dispute in the first place, but honor played a crucial role in the minds of many, if not most, of the officers who wrestled with the issues of duty and obligation in choosing sides. The feud between Franklin Buchanan and French Forrest thus took place in an environment where honor was a valued coin. But each man was also a product of the long traditions of the sea service in which rank was a public validation of one's private honor. Imputations of undeserved rank were commonly considered grounds for satisfaction long before the Confederacy was established. The lieutenants and midshipmen of the age of sail, from New England as well as the antebellum South, fought each other so frequently that dueling was almost a disease. Thus, it was the tradition of the sea service as much as the Southern *code duello* that triggered Buchanan's angry response to the four dotted lines that he believed Forrest had purposefully inserted in the Confederate *Navy Register*.

CRAIG L. SYMONDS is a professor of history at the United States Naval Academy at Annapolis and author of *Confederate Admiral: The Life and Wars of Franklin Buchanan* (Naval Institute Press, 1999) and *Stonewall of the West: Patrick Cleburne and the Civil War* (University Press of Kansas, 1997).

CHURCHILL'S LONELY CAMPAIGN

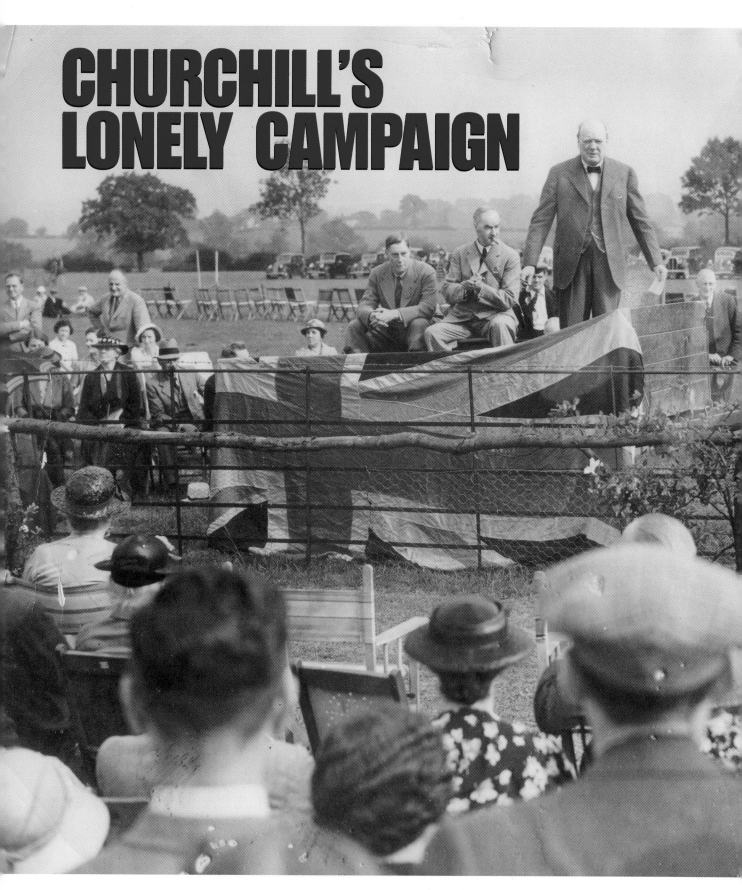

Perceiving the impending danger posed by Nazi Germany, Winston Churchill battled Britain's government and public opinion for increased military spending in the 1930s.

by Williamson Murray

Declaring that the rapidly expanding German army threatens European peace, Winston Churchill addresses a Theydon Bois, Essex, gathering on August 27, 1938.

NATIONAL ARCHIVES

The most depressing time in Winston Churchill's long life was the 1930s. It was a period during which he clearly saw the approaching Nazi danger and during which his speeches—in fact his greatest—warned a heedless polity of its reckless course. Then, after every strategic advantage enjoyed by France and Britain had been "squandered and thrown away," Churchill found himself as prime minister.

What separated Churchill from his contemporaries was his recognition from 1933 on that Nazi Germany represented a terrifying strategic and moral danger. It was in that dark combination, he believed, that the rights, traditions, and fundamental beliefs of Western civilization were already under assault. In July 1934, Churchill wrote in the *Daily Mail*:

I marvel at the complacency of ministers in the face of the frightful experiences through which we have all so newly passed. I look with wonder upon the thoughtless crowds disporting themselves in the summer sunshine, and upon this unheeding House of Commons, which seems to have no higher function than to cheer a Minister; [and all the while across the North Sea], a terrible process is astir. Germany is arming.

As a result of this understanding, there were two sides to the coin: his critique of the government's rearmament policies and his articulation of alternatives to the British government's course.

Yet one must understand that Churchill's policy of rearmament and cooperation with those nations opposed to Nazi Germany did not necessarily aim at war. It is fair to take Churchill at his word. Above all, he wished to deter Hitler and his supporters from embarking on the kind of risky foreign policy that would unleash another terrible European war. If, however, Britain and her friends could not deter Nazi Germany—and that was the grim reality, given what we know today about Hitler and his regime—then at least the West could fight the next war with some prospect of success. Through-

out his career, Churchill was a supporter of the Roman saying: "If you wish peace, then prepare for war." The 1930s certainly lived up to his fears of the consequences of not following such a path.

On rearmament, Churchill maintained a steady, and at times furious, barrage against what he viewed as the consistent failure of Prime Ministers Ramsay MacDonald, Stanley Baldwin, and Neville Chamberlain to address Britain's fundamental security needs. In April 1938, an exasperated backbencher interrupted Churchill during one of his speeches urging more air defense, crying, "How much is enough?" Churchill replied that the question reminded him of the man who received a telegram from Brazil informing him: "Your mother-in-law dead; wire instructions." The man, Churchill indicated, immediately replied: "Embalm, cremate, bury at sea. Take no chances."

But Churchill was not an unregenerate defender of high defense budgets. He had played a major role in developing the infamous ten-year rule in the early 1920s, which required that military budget estimates be based on the assumption that Britain would not be in a major war in the next ten years. The result was the general rundown of Britain's defense industries, as well as its military services. Still, one must judge Churchill's advocacy of restraints on military expenditure in the 1920s by reference to the political and strategic context of the decade. Germany was then a republic and her military shackled by the Versailles Treaty. But when the international environment underwent a drastic turn for the worse in the early 1930s, he at least recognized that Britain must fundamentally change its defense policies.

So too did the government. The argument between those in power and Churchill was over the scale of rearmament. In November 1933, with the arrival of Hitler and massive German rearmament, the cabinet authorized the Defense Requirements Committee to examine Britain's defenses. After eight months of interminable wrangling and arguments, the cabinet finally agreed on the sum of seventy-one million pounds over the next five years to repair the defense deficiencies—this at a time when Hitler had already issued blank checks to the German military. By this point, the pace of Nazi rearmament had already accelerated well beyond Britain's.

Churchill's attacks on the government's policies reflected his belief that the strategic dangers and general inadequacies in defense spending would fundamentally undermine Britain's security. To a certain extent, the government's initial response reflected its readings of the British electorate's mood and the deep hostility to any idea of rearmament throughout virtually all of British society. One must note that up to September 1938 there was no alternative to the Conservative government's position on defense—unless, of course, one accepted Labor's position that no defense was the best defense.

Kingsley Martin's column in the *New Statesman* shortly after the *Anschluss*

COLLIERS

As chancellor of the Exchequer during the 1920s, Churchill advocated restrained military budgets. At the time, however, Britain's economy was wracked by a depression and labor strikes, and the threat of war in Europe was negligible.

suggests the willful opposition to even minimal defense expenditures that the Left exhibited throughout the decade: "Today, if Mr. Chamberlain would come forward and tell us that his polity was really one not only of isolation but also of Little Englandism in which the Empire was to be given up because it could not be defended and in which military defense was to be abandoned because war would totally end civilization, we, for our part, would totally support him."

Labor's record of opposing every single defense bill through to the conscription bill of April 1939 suggests why Churchill remained so isolated, given his repeated urgings for major rearmament programs. Yet even on the Conservative side, there was enormous opposition to increased defense expenditures.

Churchill's quarrels with the government came out most clearly in the arguments over allocation of resources to the Royal Air Force (RAF). Beginning in 1934 he articulated a series of warnings that the government was missing the growing threat from German air armament. In an eloquent and, in retrospect, all too accurate speech in November 1934, he warned: "To urge preparation of defense is not to assert the imminence of war. On the contrary, if war were imminent, preparations for defense would be too late." Prime Minister Baldwin replied by assuring the House of Commons, "His Majesty's Government are determined in no condition to accept any position of inferiority with regard to what air force may be raised in Germany in the future." In fact, the government was doing little to force the pace of RAF rearmament—all the more extraordinary in view of the fact that earlier that same year Baldwin had uttered his claim that "the bomber will always get through."

Baldwin's statement began a period of obfuscation, dishonesty, and lying in the face of Churchill's attacks—one in which the government still refused to provide reasonable levels of funding to the RAF. Serving RAF officers, meanwhile, kept Churchill well informed on both the state of their service and German efforts to build up the *Luftwaffe*. He did not focus on the technical details of air rearmament due to his belief that what was crucial was that the RAF receive increased funding. In the end, the govern-

ment of Neville Chamberlain made the crucial decision in late 1937 that Britain could only afford the buildup of a fighter, as opposed to a bomber, force, but it reached that decision because fighters were cheaper, rather than based on any belief in the efficacy of air defense. Churchill's constant hammering on the lack of preparedness in the air and the importance of air defense supported what buildup did occur and provided much of the narrow margin by which Fighter Command won the Battle of Britain in 1940.

Churchill's support for specific programs for the other services was less influential. Neither army nor naval officers proved quite so willing to tattle on the government's sorry record of support. Although Churchill never expressed support for Basil Liddell Hart's ahistorical strategic concept of "limited liability"—a belief that Britain should not commit major military forces to the Continent in the case of a general war—the horrific casualty rates in France during World War I had scarred him, like his contemporaries. While recognizing that Britain would have to commit troops to the Continent in support of France in another war, he also saw that some things were better left unargued in the political and intellectual atmosphere of the 1930s. Thus, he did not argue so vehemently in favor of financial increases in the army's budget to support the French. But Churchill's larger understanding was that underfunding the overall defense budget would ensure a state of unpreparedness at the onset of hostilities that would have dark consequences on future battlefields. He was right.

The navy, largely due to the Washington Naval Treaties, seemed least threatened by a German buildup. Certainly in its own eyes it was ready to master the immediate threat. But it, too, would not be ready for the war in the North Atlantic in 1939. What Churchill failed to see were the intellectual and doctrinal weaknesses in the preparations of Britain's military forces. The army's culture and its lack of understanding of what had happened on the battlefield in the last war had already put the British out of the ground-war race even before German rearmament began in February 1933. Unfortunately,

Churchill remained blind to the systemic weaknesses in the army, and that blindness prevented him from forcing that organization to come up to the mark even by the end of World War II.

The other great issue between Churchill and virtually everyone in power in Britain in the 1930s—and most in opposition—had to do with his fundamentally different *Weltanschauung* (worldview). His beliefs were similar to those of the great Greek historian Thucydides, who had suggested that his purpose in writing a history of the Peloponnesian War was so that "these words of mine [will be] judged useful by those who want to understand clearly the events which happened in the past and which (human nature being what it its) will, at some time or other and in much the same ways, be repeated in the future."

Throughout the interwar years, Churchill was hard at work on his great histories, *The World Crisis* and *Marlborough, His Life and Times*. By writing history during so much of the 1920s and '30s, Churchill expanded his sense of the continuities and dangers of the past. The real world of human strife remained firmly in his understanding of the current world. One passage in *Marlborough*, among many, reflecting on the strategic framework within which the War of the Spanish Succession was fought, illustrates that brilliant combination of past and present in Churchill's writing and his recognition that we must see the world as it is, not as we wish it to be:

It was a war of the circumference against the center. When we reflect upon the selfish aims, the jealousies and shortcomings of the allies, upon their many divergent interests, upon the difficulties of procuring common and timely agreement upon any single necessary measure, upon the weariness, moral and physical, which drags down all prolonged human effort…we cannot regard it as strange that Louis XIV should so long have sustained his motto, "*Nec pluribus impar.*" Lying in his central station with complete control of the greatest nation of the world in one of its most remarkable ebullitions, with the power to plan far in advance, to strike now in this quarter, now in that, and above all with the certainty of complete obedience, it is little wonder how well and how long he fought. The marvel is that any force could have been found in that unequipped civilization of Europe to withstand, still less to subdue him.

Even as he evaluated the world of the 1930s, Churchill held an historical and

From 1935 to '37 Churchill's rearmament campaign targeted the fiscal policies of Prime Minister Stanley Baldwin (right). The necessity of beefing up the Royal Air Force to counter the growing Luftwaffe *was a consistent theme. Below: Hawker Hurricanes, Britain's first modern monoplane fighters, went into RAF service in early 1938, but tight budgets limited their numbers.*

RIGHT: HULTON/ARCHIVE' INSET: NATIONAL ARCHIVES

fundamentally pessimistic view of what the German threat meant to Britain. This influence thoroughly informed his views on foreign and defense policy. Those who determined Britain's response in the late 1930s did not agree. Over them, as over Churchill, hung the shadows of the Loos, the Somme, and Paschendaele. But where Churchill aimed at meeting the challenge by backing up a strong foreign policy with major rearmament programs, they chose another tack. Admittedly, British politicians and strategists confronted complex problems. Britain's economic position had weakened considerably compared to 1914, she faced a major threat to her interests in the Far East, and even the Italians were a significant challenge in the Mediterranean.

Underlying the government's policy was an unreasonable belief that international affairs had changed in fundamental ways since 1914. Strategic interests did not matter, military power would not play a significant part in the equation again, and above all, war was something that no reasonable statesman would ever consider. Appeasement, as practiced by the British governments of the late 1930s, represented an odd combination of naiveté, optimistic assessments, and a belief in the supremacy of morality in international affairs. Neville Henderson, ambassador to Berlin, best caught this mixture in a cable he sent to the foreign minister, Lord Halifax, in May 1938 as the political struggle over the future of Czechoslovakia's predominantly German Sudetenland began heating up:

Yet even when I try to imagine that which I feel in my heart to be inevitable and evolutional is neither, and when I think in terms of British interests only, regardless of right or wrong, I still feel that however repugnant, dangerous, and troublesome the result may be or may seem likely to be, the truest British interest is to come down on the side of the highest moral principles. And the only lastingly right moral principle is self-determination. The British Empire is built upon it and we cannot deny it without incalculable prejudice to something which is of infinitely greater importance to the world than apprehensions of the German menace.

Three months later, as the Czech crisis was exploding, Henderson wrote Halifax:

The memory of the Great War's horrors and the belief that no reasonable statesman would consider unleashing another such terrible conflict dominated Western European thinking during the interwar years and facilitated Nazi Germany's aggression in the late 1930s. Top: German troops, assisted by sympathetic Austrian police, tear down a frontier barrier as Adolf Hitler's forces pour into Austria on March 12, 1938. Above: German soldiers advance through the Czech capital of Prague in a halftrack during March 1939.

"Personally I just sit and pray for one thing, namely that Lord Runciman [head of a diplomatic mission to Czechoslovakia] will live up to the role of the impartial British liberal statesman. I cannot believe that he will allow himself to be influenced by ancient history or even arguments about strategic frontiers and economics in preference to high moral principles."

As the great twentieth-century historian of Eastern Europe Louis Namier has pointed out, the 1,250 pages of published documents on British foreign policy dealing with the Czech crisis over the summer of 1938 contain not a single reference to the strategic and military impact of abandoning Czechoslovakia without a fight and the consequences that such an action would have on the European military balance of power in succeeding years. Since the opening up of the British cabinet documents in the early 1970s, we know that this crucial question does not appear in cabinet discussions until September 16, 1938, when Oliver Stanley, president of the Board of Trade, asked what the results of a surrender of Czechoslovakia might be.

In fact, Chamberlain and his supporters in the cabinet were not afraid of losing a war to Germany in 1938. As Halifax told the cabinet in mid-September 1938, he "had no doubt that if we were involved in war now, we should win it after a long time." Halifax then, however, continued on to add what lay at the heart of the appeasers' objection to a hard policy toward Germany—an approach that might result in war. He "could not feel that we were justified in embarking on an action which could result in such untold suffering." Consequently, the result was a consistent "best case" analysis of German intentions, goals, and behavior—a state of mind that all too often slipped over into the intellectual dishonesty exhibited in an entry in the diary of Geoffrey Dawson, editor of the London *Times*, that he was engaged in a constant battle to take out everything in the paper that might hurt German sensibilities.

Moreover, reinforcing the thrust of British policy throughout the late 1930s was a military "worst casing" of the strategic situation. In some instances, such as Chamberlain's charge to the chiefs of staff for a European evaluation done in reaction to the *Anschluss*, the government deliberately loaded the dice to encourage gloomy assessments of the strategic situation. But the chiefs of staff hardly needed encouragement in 1938 to paint a dark picture of British and Allied prospects should war occur. In the March 1938 appreciation, they commented:

We conclude that no pressure that we and our possible allies can bring to bear, either by sea, on land or in the air could prevent Germany from invading and overrunning Bohemia and from inflicting a decisive defeat of the Czechoslovakian army....In the world situation today it seems to us...Italy and Japan would seize the opportunity to further their own ends and that in consequence the problem we have to envisage is not that of a limited European war only, but of a World

A stern-faced Churchill and British Foreign Minister Lord Halifax walk to Parliament several weeks after Germany's annexation of Austria. The British government had already concluded that, according to Halifax, "Czechoslovakia is not worth the bones of a single British grenadier."

War. On this situation we reported as follows some four months only:—"Without overlooking the assistance we should hope to obtain from France and possibly other allies, we cannot foresee the time when our defense forces will be strong enough to safeguard our territory, trade and vital interests against Germany, Italy, and Japan simultaneously."

A careful reading of the military and strategic evidence, however, indicates that the military situation in 1938 was far more favorable to the Allies than what they were to face in 1939. Even a substantial number of Germany's senior military leaders felt the same.

Churchill remained opposed to the government's and the military's assessments for realistic reasons. He understood the nature of the Nazi regime and recognized that it represented an enormous ideological threat, although he phrased his understanding more in terms of good and evil than in terms of ideology. Consequently, he understood what his contemporaries refused to see: There was no chance of reaching a long-term accommodation with Hitler or the Nazis. Any agreement could only result in

undermining Britain's values, traditions, and moral position. On the military side, he evaluated the strategic balance more favorably than did the chiefs of staff.

In the end it was a good thing that Churchill remained out of office during the 1930s. There is no doubt that he sought office during this period. He was particularly upset that he failed to get the position of minister for the coordination of defense in 1936. Baldwin appointed the little-known and unsuited Sir Thomas Inskip to that position, an appointment Churchill accurately described as the most astonishing since Caligula had appointed his horse consul of Rome. The larger issue, however, in view of the political realities and limitations of the 1930s (and not in view of what we know about the results) is the question of what Churchill could have achieved that the governments of the time did not. As a member of the government in 1937 and 1938—given political attitudes within the cabinet, particularly after Chamberlain became prime minister—Churchill would have had little room to maneuver in trying to expand defense spending. Moreover, as a member of the government, Churchill would have had to carry the opprobrium of defending the government's defense expenditures in public.

Much of the argument over defense in the late 1930s rested on the capability of the British economy to support a sustained program of rearmament. British governments displayed extraordinary concern throughout the period about the country's financial position—a reasonable attitude, considering the 1931 financial panic and continuing difficulties over Britain's balance of payments. Chamberlain warned the cabinet in spring 1937, shortly before he became prime minister, that he

could not accept the question at issue [the services' request for increased defense spending] as being a purely military matter. Other considerations entered into it. The country was being asked to maintain a larger navy than had been the case for very many years; a great air force, which was a new arm altogether; and, in addition, an army for use on the Continent—as well as the facilities for producing munitions which would be required not only for our forces but also for our allies.

Chamberlain's path as both chancellor of the Exchequer and prime minister represented a consistent effort to minimize British defense expenditures, at least through March 1939. Certainly, the political consensus through much of the period agreed with his economic and diplomatic analysis. It is worth noting, however, that there were elements even within the Treasury that believed that Britain could have supported higher levels of rearmament.

Admittedly, even as prime minister Churchill would have found it difficult to push much beyond Chamberlain's armament programs—at least until late summer 1938—given the attitudes within the Conservative Party, not to mention the country as a whole. In fact, either a strong rearmament policy or an adventurous foreign policy—or the two in combination—might well have fractured the British polity and made the kind of unity demanded by a great world war impossible. Up till September 1938, Chamberlain's foreign policy was defensible in terms of British popular attitudes. However, the prime minister stepped off into disaster when he refused to recognize that Hitler's behavior in the summer and fall of 1938 had revealed the darker aims and goals of the Nazi regime.

But having come face to face with Nazi intransigence and truculence in the period before the Munich conference, Chamberlain had crumbled. The eventual result was the tragic and disastrous surrender of Czechoslovakia at the end of September 1938. Throughout that summer and fall, Churchill saw the terrible strategic and military consequences of the government's course. He could badger the ministers, but he could not change the policy. The greatest speech of his career came in his chilling depiction in early October 1938 of what the Western powers had abandoned to the Nazis at Munich. A few short paragraphs provide all the reader needs to know about Churchill's separation from the perceived wisdom of the British nation at large—a gulf the furious reception that most of the House of Commons gave to his dire warnings further underlines:

All is over. Silent, mournful, abandoned, broken Czechoslovakia recedes into the darkness.

She has suffered in every respect by her association with France, under whose guidance and policy she has been actuated for so long…. Every position has been undermined and abandoned on specious and plausible excuses.

I do not grudge our loyal, brave people, who were ready to do their duty no matter what the cost, who never flinched under the strain of last week, the natural, spontaneous outburst of joy and relief when they learned that the hard ordeal would no longer be required of them at the moment; but they should know the truth….They should know that we have

Despite the shock of Hitler's occupation of Prague, Chamberlain still refused to bring Churchill into the cabinet.

sustained a defeat without a war, the consequences of which will travel with us along our road; they should know that we have passed an awful milestone in our history, when the whole equilibrium of Europe has been deranged and that the terrible words have for the time been spoken against the Western Democracies: "Thou art weighed in the balance and found wanting." And do not suppose that this is the end. This is the beginning of the reckoning. This is only the first sip, the first foretaste of a bitter cup….

The collapse of the Munich agreement with Hitler's seizure of Bohemia and Moravia in March 1939 restored Churchill's political position after the darkness of a wilderness that had lasted almost a decade. What was particularly disastrous for Britain's prospects in the coming war was the fact that Chamberlain had done virtually nothing to accelerate British military preparations between September 1938 and March 1939. Outside of construction of a few escort vessels and extension of contracts for fighter production from 1941 into '42, his government refused to address any of the substantial weaknesses that had appeared during the mobilization occasioned by the Czech crisis. In the end, there had been no speeding up the rearmament effort.

Despite the shock of Hitler's occupation of Prague in March 1939, Chamberlain still refused to bring Churchill into the cabinet. One suspects that the prime minister had two reasons: a fear of Churchill's dominating personality and a belief that Churchill's inclusion in the cabinet would represent to many in and outside of Germany that Britain regarded war as inevitable.

After March 1939, Chamberlain and Halifax were more interested in deterring Germany and cutting her off diplomatically than in creating a viable military coalition to defeat the Nazis. Their failure to approach the Soviet Union and the distribution of guarantees to the states of Eastern Europe, none of which France and Britain had the slightest hope of supporting with military force, suggest an unwillingness to face the hard realities of a fast-approaching war. From what we now know of Soviet policy, there was no chance that the West and the Soviets might have reached an accommodation, especially after the Germans recognized that they could make a deal with the Soviets. But the guarantees throughout Eastern Europe were strategic madness.

Churchill welcomed the government's change of direction but was soon appalled by its attitudes toward Russia. He also recognized the necessity for a stand in Eastern Europe. But, again, the lack of realism in much of Chamberlain's policy—at least what Churchill knew of the government's policies—could not have pleased him. His cutting comment on the guarantee to Poland in his memoirs suggests the degree of his differences:

And now, when every one of these aids and advantages has been squandered and thrown away, Great Britain advances, leading France by the hand, to guarantee the integrity of Poland—to that very Poland which with hyena appetite had only six months before joined in the pillage and destruction of the Czechoslovak state. There was sense in fighting for Czechoslovakia in 1938 when the German army could put barely a dozen trained divisions on the Western Front, when the French with nearly sixty or seventy divisions could most certainly have rolled forward across the Rhine or into the Ruhr. But this had all been judged unreasonable, rash, below the level of modern intellectual

Soldiers and panzers of Germany's rejuvenated Wehrmacht *demonstrate battle tactics during the September 1938 Nazi Party rally in Nuremburg. Churchill understood that, in addition to being a military threat, Nazi Germany represented an ideological threat with which no compromise could be reached.*

broke out, encourage him to enter the conflict at Germany's side? For one of the few times in the 1930s, the Chamberlain government got the issue right. The prime minister himself argued in a meeting of the Foreign Policy Committee that there were important advantages in having the Italians on Germany's side during any war. Nevertheless, in the end the British chiefs of staff talked the government out of one of the few sensible strategic courses that it had considered during the 1930s. The military's arguments rested on entirely specious grounds—that Italy might "be in a position to hit us more effectively at the outset than we can hit her...."

The difference that Churchill might have made in the debate over Italy is suggested by his participation, as first lord of the Admiralty, in the debates after the start of war. In early October 1939, there arose a question as to whether the Allies should mine the Norwegian leads, or coastal waters, to prevent transshipment of Swedish ore through neutral waters to Germany. Not surprisingly, Churchill backed this course. In December the chiefs of staff raised objections because they wished to persuade the Scandinavians to allow a major movement of Allied forces across Norway and Sweden to support the Finns. Churchill's devastating one-page reply to such nonsense underlines why his leadership, with its extraordinary grasp and understanding, was so essential to British victory in World War II:

The self-contained minor operation of stopping the ore from Narvik and Oxelsund [namely the mining of the Norwegian leads] must not be tried because it would jeopardize the larger plan. The larger plan [getting Norway and Sweden to invite the Allies in] must not be attempted unless Norway and Sweden cooperate. Not only must they not resist militarily or adopt a purely passive attitude, but must actively cooperate....But is there any

thought or morality. Yet now at last the two Western Democracies declared themselves ready to stake their lives upon the territorial integrity of Poland. History which we are told is mainly the record of crimes, follies and miseries of mankind, may be scoured and ransacked to find a parallel to this sudden and complete reversal of five or six years' policy of easy going placatory appeasement, and its transformation almost overnight into a readiness to accept an obviously imminent war on far worse conditions and on the greatest scale.

What is apparent in the course of British policy in 1939 is that two major assessments of Germany—the political and the military—had undergone substantial change since Munich. On the political level, the government had revised its picture of the Nazi regime and of Hitler in particular. Churchill agreed fully with the change in political assessment, although unlike the government, he recognized that war was inevitable.

But on the strategic side, the British military downgraded its estimates of Germany's military and economic ability to meet the demands of another great world war, while they were increasing their estimates of their own potential. Two factors explain the change. First, British strategic intelligence, even as the Czech crisis lurched to its end in September 1938, had picked up how badly prepared militarily and economically the

Germans had been to meet war in fall 1938. Throughout the winter of 1938-39, a flood of intelligence confirmed that Germany's situation had been dangerously weak in the fall. The second factor was that after the German occupation of Prague, the firestorm of political anger in Britain forced the government to begin a massive program of rearmament to meet the Nazi threat. The prospects of that program lifted much of the British military's forebodings as to the situation. It should not have.

Over the summer of 1939, the Chamberlain government continued making crucial decisions on the basis of general ignorance of strategic factors. Its record thus far had not been stellar; it did not improve in the last months before war. Here is where one suspects that Churchill might have contributed much to these desperate prewar debates, the unfortunate outcomes of which resulted in Nazi Germany's escape from its strategic vulnerabilities in the first seven months of the war. Churchill's unrivaled ability to strip faulty reasoning from the body of argument and to plunge through to the heart of the matter might well have pushed the Western powers on a more realistic course.

One of the crucial arguments in the summer of 1939 revolved around the Italian problem: Should Britain and France appease Benito Mussolini or, if war

Above: Prime Minister Neville Chamberlain is greeted by Adolf Hitler in September 1939—only hours before signing the Munich agreement that gave Germany the Czech Sudetenland. Right: Relieved that war has been averted, Chamberlain addresses member of the press upon his return to Britain.

prospect of Sweden and Norway actually co-operating with us of their own free will to bring about a series of operations which as is well set out in their [chiefs of staff] paper will a) ruin the trade of their ironfield and the shipping which carries it; b) involve them in a war with Germany; c) expose the whole southern part of both countries to German invasion and occupation? Left to themselves they will certainly refuse, and, if pressed diplomatically, they will protest loudly to the world. Thus, the minor operation is knocked out for the sake of the bigger, and the bigger is declared only practicable upon conditions that will not occur.

A combination of Halifax's opposition to strong actions against neutral powers and the chiefs of staffs' prestige thwarted Churchill's support for the mining operation in the winter. Eventually, immediately before Germany's April 9, 1940, invasion of Scandinavia, the operation went forward. Consequently, the British provided the Germans with an excuse for their aggression while gaining little military advantage because the mining came so late.

It was in his ability to recognize the heart of the argument that Churchill was to be such a great war leader. Much of the nonsense that characterized argu-ments put forward by the government's military advisers in the late 1930s never passed muster under Churchill's alert and penetrating gaze during the war. In 1938 this would have made little difference, even had Churchill been in the cabinet; Chamberlain and his supporters had made up their mind on the basis of the political assessment that the men in Berlin were reasonable individuals.

In summer 1939, however, Churchill might have made some considerable difference in a cabinet more open to strategic or military direction. Lord Ismay best summed up Churchill's abilities as a strategist in a letter that he wrote to the new theater commander in the Middle East, General Claude Auchinleck:

The idea that he [Churchill] was rude, arrogant, and self-seeking was entirely wrong. He was none of those things. He was certainly frank in speech and writing, but he expected others to be equally frank with him. To a young brigadier from Middle East Headquarters who had asked him if he could speak freely, he replied: "Of course. We are not here to pay each other compliments."...He had a considerable respect for the trained military mind, but refused to subscribe to the idea that generals were infallible or had any monopoly on the military art. He was not a gambler, but never shrank from taking a calculated risk if the situation so demanded....

Another one of Churchill's military advisers characterized the change from Chamberlain to Churchill in the following terms: "The days of mere 'coordination' were out for good and all....We were now going to get direction, leadership with a snap in it." Churchill himself accurately remarked that the strategic decision-making system under his predecessors had represented "the maximum of study and the minimum of action. It was all very well to say that everything had been thought of. The crux of the matter was—had anything been done?"

Over the summer of 1939, Churchill waited for the war that he knew was coming. As he told an American audience in a sarcastic speech broadcast from Britain:

Holiday time, ladies and gentlemen! Holiday time, my friends across the Atlantic! Holiday time, when the summer calls the toilers of all countries for an all too brief spell from the offices and mills....

Let me look back—let me see. How did we spend our summer holidays twenty-five years ago? Why those were the very days when the German advance guards were breaking into Belgium and trampling down its people....

But perhaps we are wrong. Perhaps our memory deceives us. Dr. Geobbels and his Propaganda Ministry have their own version of what happened twenty-five years ago. To hear them talk, you would suppose that it was Belgium that invaded Germany! There they were, these peaceful Prussians, gathering in their harvests, when this wicked Belgium—set on by England and the Jews—fell upon them....

But to come back to the hush I said was hanging over Europe. What kind of hush is it? Alas! it is the hush of suspense, and in many lands it is the hush of fear. Listen! No, listen carefully; I think I hear something—yes, there it is quite clear. Don't you hear it? It is the tramp of armies crunching the gravel of the parade-grounds, splashing through rain soaked fields, the tramp of two million German soldiers and more than a million Italians—"going on maneuvers"—yes, only on maneuvers! Of course it's only maneuvers— just like last year. After all, the dictators must train their soldiers. They could scarcely do less in common prudence, when the Danes, the Dutch, the Swiss, the Albanians—and of course the Jews—may leap out upon them at any moment to rob them of their living space, and make them sign another paper to say who began it.

Churchill's time soon came. But Chamberlain waited until the actual outbreak of war with Germany's invasion of Poland and the declaration of war by Britain before he allowed Churchill to re-enter the charmed circle of decision makers in the cabinet. On September 3 he was named first lord of the Admiralty. By this point, Churchill's reputation was such that, given the accuracy of his predictions and warnings, not even the failure of the Norwegian campaign—which was not his greatest moment—could prevent him from assuming the leadership of his nation in the dark days of May 1940.

How to evaluate the years in the wilderness? Churchill, indeed, waged a lonely crusade against the revealed wisdom of most of Britain's literate society. His position on the outside allowed him to express his opinions with a freedom that would not have been possible within the cabinet. Moreover, through to the Czech crisis, there was little chance that the British govern-

After Germany's occupation of Prague, Churchill's warnings of German aggression were validated. However, despite public pressure, as illustrated in this political cartoon, Chamberlain refrained from appointing Churchill to his government until after the outbreak of war.

ment could have pursued a stronger course in either foreign policy or in rearmament, given national attitudes, without the considerable danger of splitting the nation.

Where British policy sorely missed Churchill's wisdom was in the post-Munich period. Through March 1939, the government refused any speedup in its rearmament programs. The year between Munich and the outbreak of war was one that Britain largely wasted and of which the Germans took full advantage. Moreover, Churchill's absence from strategic debates after March 1939 drove British and French strategy toward a supine unwillingness to undertake any military action, despite the considerable weaknesses still plaguing the German military and economy. As a result, Germany escaped its predicament, and in the May 1940 campaign in the West completely overturned the European balance of power, at least for the short run. But Churchill's prestige, gained in his lonely battles of the 1930s, provided him the persona to persuade the British people to stand alone after the fall of France.

Churchill's prewar efforts, then, had gone for naught—his own people had not listened. Might his course have prevented war? That, of course, is one of the great imponderables of the 1930s. The evidence available certainly suggests that nothing could have avoided war except abject surrender. But the course

that Churchill advocated carried with it a real level of military and strategic preparation that might at least have enabled the West to win the conflict at less cost, whatever the nature or the timing of the war that broke out.

As for that lonely fight against the tide of public opinion, the intellectual elite, and the masters of his own party, perhaps only the words of seventeenth-century poet John Milton capture the courage and tenacity of Churchill's struggle against those who knew better:

So spake the Seraph Abdiel faithful found
Among the faithless, faithful only hee;
Among innumerable false, unmov'd
Unshak'n, unseduc'd, unterrifi'd
His Loyalty he kept, his Love, his Zeal;
Nor number, nor example with him
    wrought
To swerve from truth, or change his
    constant mind
Though single. From amidst them forth
    he pass'd,
Long way through hostile scorn, which
    he sustain'd
Superior, nor of violence fear'd aught;
And with retorted scorn his back he turn'd.

WILLIAMSON MURRAY is an *MHQ* contributing editor and a professor emeritus of history at The Ohio State University. His many books include *A War to Be Won: Fighting the Second World War* (Harvard University Press, 2000), which he co-authored with Allan R. Millett.

OPPOSING VIEWS

Pearl Harbor Responsibilities

Who was responsible for the lack of defense readiness on the island of Oahu that tragic Sunday morning in 1941? As the American people come to grips with another tragic "day of infamy," and the debate rages once again over a failure of U.S. intelligence and lack of preparedness, that question has taken on additional import.

Nearly sixty years after Japan's attack on Pearl Harbor, Congress effectively exonerated the senior U.S. Navy and Army commanders in Hawaii at the time, Admiral Husband E. Kimmel and General Walter C. Short, by describing their performance of duty as "competently and professionally" executed. In an article in the Winter 2001 issue of MHQ, Frederic Borch disagreed with the lawmakers and accepted the official consensus found in the ten Pearl Harbor investigations conducted between 1941 and 1996. The general understanding among most of these probes was that some degree of blame should be assigned to Kimmel and Short.

Almost immediately after its publication, Borch's article drew thoughtful and instructive criticism from the admiral's grandson, Thomas K. Kimmel, Jr. Given the importance of this debate, we decided to forego the usual letter to the editor and author's response in favor of a more lengthy and informative arrangement by asking Kimmel to write a concise challenge essay and requesting a rebuttal from Borch. We are delighted to offer the results of these two gentlemen's labors and hope our readers agree that their arguments add interesting dimensions to the concept of command and responsibility.

Unfairly Shouldering the Blame
by Thomas K. Kimmel, Jr.

For sixty years the reputations of two honorable men—Rear Adm. Husband E. Kim- mel, former commander of the Pacific Fleet, and Maj. Gen. Walter C. Short, former commander of the U.S. Army Hawaiian Department—have lain in humiliating ruin in the wake of the Japanese attack on Pearl Harbor. The Officer Personnel Act of 1947 allowed for a qualified military officer to retire at his highest rank held in World War II. Only two such officers were not allowed to so retire—Kimmel and Short. Finally, in October 1999 Congress approved and President Bill Clinton signed a request for the posthumous reinstatement of Kimmel and Short to their highest-held World War II ranks, four-star and three-star rank, respectively, and stated that these two officers had performed their duties "competently and professionally."

Assuming that President George W. Bush chooses to honor Congress' request, justice will have been accomplished at long last. I will herein describe the case for advancement of these two commanders, and in so doing, respond to the *MHQ* article "Guilty as Charged?" (Volume 13, Number 2), which argued that the commanders were indeed responsible for the disaster at Pearl Harbor.

The author of the article, Colonel Frederic L. Borch III, served as the army's representative during the most recent review of the matter, a probe headed by Department of Defense Undersecretary Edwin S. Dorn in 1995. His report, known as the Dorn Report, was the first by a government tribunal to acknowledge that responsibility for the Pearl Harbor disaster should not fall solely on the shoulders of Admiral Kimmel and General Short, but rather should be broadly shared. The report, however, concluded that the two officers should not be advanced in rank to full admiral and lieutenant general. Borch maintains that, as the senior officers in charge, Kimmel and Short did not perform their duties and made serious errors in judgment and therefore must "shoulder much of the blame for what happened."

Many eminent naval experts disagree with his assessment. The five greatest admirals of World War II, five modern-day admirals, and President Franklin D. Roosevelt's official naval historian, Samuel Eliot Morison, all agree that Kimmel was treated unfairly. World War II Admirals William "Bull" Halsey, Ernest King, Thomas Kinkaid, Chester Nimitz, and Raymond Spruance made it clear that they believed that Kimmel was singled out as a scapegoat and unjustly punished. Later naval leaders—including four chiefs of Naval Operations, two heads of the Joint Chiefs of Staff, and Admirals William Crowe, James Holloway, Thomas Moorer, Carlisle Trost, and Elmo Zumwalt—have agreed. All expressly supported remedial action for the two officers in language now elevated to law.

But more important than the veritable who's who of naval history supporting Kimmel are the facts. Let us examine them in more detail, keeping in mind that Admiral Kimmel was never charged with dereliction of duty or errors of judgment (or anything else) by a court or government agency that afforded him the opportunity to defend his name.

Ten U.S. tribunals have examined the Pearl Harbor disaster. Nine of them, including a 1946 hearing before a joint congressional committee, were held while Kimmel and Short were alive. But most important, only one, the 1944 Naval Court of Inquiry, accorded the admiral the right to call and to cross-examine witnesses—the most fundamental of due-process rights. That tribunal unanimously and completely exonerated Admiral Kimmel of dereliction of duty charges, approved of his force dispositions in view of the information he had, and found that he committed no errors of judgment, while severely criticizing his superior, Chief of Naval Operations Admiral Harold Stark, for not keeping Kimmel properly informed. The Naval Court of Inquiry was also the only tribunal

whose members all had the professional competence to judge Kimmel's naval performance, as all three judging admirals had held high commands at sea.

The importance of restating the uniqueness of the Naval Court of Inquiry was underscored at the tenth tribunal in 1995. The navy's general counsel, in the presence of but without objection from the secretary of the navy and the deputy secretary of defense, stated that "…the official position of the [Navy] Department today [is that]….Admiral Kimmel enjoyed due process before the [joint congressional] Committee…he had the right to call and question witnesses."

This was absolutely incorrect. Kimmel did not have the right to call or to question witnesses before the joint congressional panel. If the general counsel of the navy, the secretary of the navy, and the deputy secretary of defense did not know this important fact at a hearing to specifically address the issue of fairness to the admiral, it bears repeating here. Unfortunately, Colonel Borch was not present, to my knowledge, when the general counsel made his regrettable remarks, which remain uncorrected in the official record, virtually ensuring future prejudicial error to Kimmel, as well as to Short.

This leaves us with the question: Why not name those responsible? The Dorn Report, for the first time, recognized that Kimmel and Short were not solely responsible for the defeat at Pearl Harbor. Although the report charged other, unnamed persons with responsibility, it did not name them. It also did not consider that they might be more blamable than Kimmel and Short or the effect that their errors might have had on errors attributed to Admiral Kimmel and General Short. Admiral Spruance believed that the real reason why Kimmel and Short were singled out for blame in the first place was so that others equally and more responsible would

not have to be named. The Battle of Midway commander said: "I have always felt that Kimmel [was] held responsible for Pearl Harbor in order that the American people might have no reason to lose confidence in their Government in Washington. This was probably justifiable under the circumstances at that time, but it does not justify forever damning [this] fine officer."

Command accountability and responsibility, it is important to remember, are not synonymous with blame. The Dorn Report stated that "A commander has plenary responsibility for the welfare of the people under his command…." But the Army Pearl Harbor Board found an exception and said in its top-secret report:

…where information has a vital bearing upon actions to be taken by field commanders, and this information cannot be disclosed by the War Department to its field commanders, it is incumbent upon the War Department then to assume the responsibility for specific directions to the theater commanders. This is an exception to the admirable policy of the War Department of decentralized and complete responsibility upon the competent field commanders….Short got neither form of assistance from the War Department.

Arguing in the abstract and blindly applying absolute responsibility to the field commander, it must then follow that the twelve commanders of the ships sunk at Pearl Harbor must each somehow be blamed for the loss of his ship. In the recent case of USS *Cole*, neither the ship's skipper nor the commander in chief Central Command was blamed. So much for plenary responsibility.

Of course, commanding officers are responsible and accountable, but these points obscure the important questions: Who is to blame? Who should be punished? An analogous case is that of the captain of USS *Indianapolis*, which was sunk

by a Japanese torpedo in July 1945. In a recent decision the navy reversed its adverse finding of blame against the accountable—but blameless and scapegoated—captain and posthumously exonerated him.

What did they know? When did they know it? What did they do about it? In asking these questions about Pearl Harbor, the high command in Washington confined and continues to confine "they" to Kimmel and Short. Let us expand "they" to include the rest of the appropriate leadership—especially the Washington high command.

The U.S. government and military possessed solid intelligence about Japanese plans before December 7, 1941. According to the Army Pearl Harbor Board:

Information from informers and other means as to the activities of our potential enemy and their intentions in the negotiations between the United States and Japan was in possession of the State, War and Navy Departments in November and December of 1941. Such agencies had a reasonably complete disclosure of the Japanese plans and intentions, and were in a position to know what were the Japanese potential moves that were scheduled by them against the Untied States. Therefore, Washington was in possession of essential facts as to the enemy's intentions….This information showed clearly that war was inevitable and late in November absolutely imminent. It clearly demonstrated the necessity of resorting to every trading act possible to defer the ultimate day of breach of relations to give the Army and Navy time to prepare for the eventualities of war.

Intelligence from "other means" undoubtedly refers to Magic, the code name for secretly deciphered Japanese diplomatic and spy communications. Magic, which also contained military intelligence, was explained by the head of army intelligence and the joint congressional committee chief assistant counsel as "…the most reli-

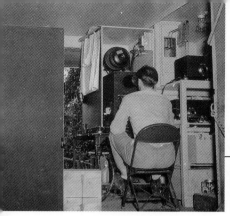

A SCR 270 mobile radio detecting and ranging (radar) set and aerial. On December 7, 1941, six SCR 270s were in operation on Oahu. Critics claim that Short failed to use these early-warning assets properly and considered radar to be "for training purposes only," despite his knowledge that it had helped win the Battle of Britain.

able and authentic information which the War Department was receiving as to Japanese intentions and activities…and that some of these messages…were not of a diplomatic nature, they were of a military nature." None of the intelligence from Magic, however, was forwarded to Kimmel or Short.

According to Colonel Borch, "…the Magic messages would have provided no useful tactical information to Kimmel and Short." The decoded Japanese messages, however, included:

• A bomb-plot message
• 147 ships-in-harbor messages (sixty-eight applied to Pearl Harbor—one of which, left undecoded before the attack, said there was still "considerable opportunity to take advantage for a surprise attack" on Pearl Harbor)
• time-of-delivery messages
• deceit-plan messages
• the ultimatum-delivery message, which gave the War Department its only notification that Secretary of State Cordell Hull had submitted a diplomatic note to Japan on November 26, 1941
• the ultimatum-response message, which notified the War Department that Japan considered Secretary Hull's proposal to be humiliating.

In short, Magic provided information indicating the time of the attack, the place of the attack, the planned deceit to cover the attack, and the motivation of the attack—all of which is tactical information. The potential usefulness of such information to Kimmel and Short was enormous. However, the two commanders did not receive any of it. Kimmel had formally asked for all vital information; had been assured that he would have it; appeared to be receiving it, for he did receive some useless Magic messages; and estimated the situation based on it. Admiral Kimmel and General Short were deprived of the most important information and positively misled.

Alfred McCormack, a New York lawyer recruited by Secretary of War Henry L. Stimson after the attack to straighten out perceived shortcomings in Magic distribution, reported that "When the sudden attack on Pearl Harbor occurred, it became apparent that the event had been clearly foreshadowed in the Japanese traffic of 1941."

According to Fleet Admiral Halsey, U.S. commanders' foreknowledge of the Magic intelligence would have resulted in different ship deployments:

Had we known of Japan's minute and continued interest in the exact location and movement of our ships in Pearl Harbor, as indicated in the 'MAGIC Messages,' it is only logical that we would have concentrated our thoughts on meeting the practical certainty of an attack on Pearl Harbor. I am sure I would have protested the movement of my Task Force to Wake Island in late November and early December. I am also sure no protest would have been necessary; because if Kimmel had possessed this intelligence, he would not have ordered that movement.

Army Major Henry Clausen, who conducted a 1944-45 investigation, concluded that "The proximate cause for the disaster at Pearl Harbor was an unworkable system of military intelligence…." If so, who was responsible for making the system of military intelligence unworkable?

On February 18, 1941, seventeen days after he took command of the Pacific Fleet, Kimmel wrote to Admiral Stark, chief of Naval Operations:

I have recently been told by an officer fresh from Washington that ONI [the Office of Naval Intelligence] considers it the function of Operations [the Office of Naval War Plans] to furnish the Commander-in-Chief [Kimmel] with information of a secret nature. I have heard also that Operations considers the responsibility for furnishing the same type of

information to be that of ONI. I do not know that we have missed anything, but if there is any doubt as to whose responsibility it is to keep the Commander-in-Chief fully informed with pertinent reports on subjects that should be of interest to the Fleet, will you kindly fix that responsibility so that there will be no misunderstanding?"

Stark replied to Kimmel on March 22, 1941: "With reference to your postscript on the subject of…responsibility for the furnishing of secret information to OincUS [officer-in-charge United States Fleet, i.e., Kimmel]. [Chief of Naval Intelligence Alan] Kirk informs me that ONI is fully aware of its responsibility in keeping you adequately informed."

Four days later Kimmel responded to Admiral Stark:

The Commander-in-Chief Pacific Fleet is in a very difficult position. He is far removed from the seat of government….He is…not informed as to the policy…reflected in current events….[It] is suggested that it be made a cardinal principle that the Commander-in-Chief Pacific Fleet be immediately informed of all important developments as they occur and by the quickest secure means available.

Kimmel clearly wanted "secret information" about the Japanese. The director of the navy's War Plans Division, Admiral Richmond Turner, led others to believe that Kimmel was receiving Magic intelligence. A month before the attack, Admiral Frank Beatty, Secretary of the Navy Franklin Knox's aide, asked Turner, "Is Admiral Kimmel getting these 'MAGIC messages'? Turner replied: "Beatty, of course, he is. He has the same 'magic' setup we have here."

During the joint congressional committee investigation, General Counsel William Mitchell asked Admiral Stark, "Who was it that told you that they had a system out in Honolulu or Pearl Harbor of decoding and decrypting Jap messages?" Stark's reply: "Admiral Turner."

During the panel's hearings, when Turner was asked if he told Stark that Kimmel was receiving Magic information, he answered: "Yes, sir, on three occasions....I asked Admiral Noyes [chief of Naval Communications] about it and so reported to Admiral Stark." However, when the Naval Court of Inquiry asked Noyes, "Did you ever inform the Chief of War Plans Division, Captain Turner, that the Commander of the Pacific Fleet was decrypting intelligence information of a character similar to that which you were receiving in the Navy Department [Magic]?," his answer was "No."

Even Chief of Staff General George Marshall went on the record with his own denial. During the joint committee hearings he stated that he "was not aware" that intelligence was being withheld from Hawaii's G-2. Instead of denying knowledge of Kimmel not receiving intelligence, Director of Naval Intelligence Theodore Wilkinson reported in January 1942 to a commission headed by Supreme Court Justice Owen Roberts that Kimmel had received the same information that they had in Washington. In the words of British historian John Costello, this "...was so misleading as to be a deliberate lie." Turner and Stark acquiesced to Wilkinson's misstatement. Marshall provided similar misleading information to the Clausen investigation.

According to Admiral Harry E. Yarnell, former commander in chief of the Asiatic Fleet: "Stark and Marshall could have raised their reputations greatly by candidly admitting that their failure to send vital information to Pearl Harbor was the cause of the disaster. Yet they tried to defend themselves by failures of memory and the absurd stand that Short and Kimmel had all the information that was necessary."

Colonel Borch wrote that "...no punitive action of any kind was taken against [Kimmel or Short]....they never suffered any serious punishment." The Roberts Commission, however, proclaimed Kimmel and Short "solely responsible" for Japan's successful attack on Pearl Harbor through "dereliction of duty," which is a crime today. This proclamation remained unchallenged for years. The Navy Department did not rescind its "solely responsible" allegation against Kimmel until 1995, twenty-eight years after the admiral died. The navy has never rescinded its "dereliction" allegation against Kimmel, even though the joint congressional committee investigation put that allegation to rest for both Kimmel and Short in 1946. The Department of the Army has not rescinded its "solely responsible" or its "dereliction" allegation against Short, who died in 1949. Under stress resulting from similar allegations, Captain Charles B. McVay, skipper of ill-fated USS *Indianapolis*, committed suicide in 1968.

Admiral Kimmel and General Short dedicated their lives to duty, honor, and country. Both had long, exemplary careers. Each proved on numerous occasions a willingness to die for his country—but not to be humiliated by it. To these conscientious men of integrity, to be singled out as the only qualified U.S. officers not advanced to their highest held World War II ranks was severe punishment indeed.

It has been claimed that Kimmel and Short were not forced to retire at reduced ranks. The idea that they wanted to retire under the circumstances is absurd. The fact that they did so is a testament only to their loyalty to the country and to the war effort. They were forced to retire as a matter of fact, if not as a matter of law. Clearly the Roosevelt administration wanted them to retire, in spite of their pleas for reassignment. In Kimmel's case the navy did more than retire him against his wishes, it tried to force him to leave his retirement job at the Harris Engineering Company by threatening the company with loss of navy business if Kimmel's employment there continued.

Less than two months after the Pearl Harbor raid, Supreme Court Justice Roberts propagated the myth of Kimmel and Short's culpability when he stated in his report that they were solely responsible for the success of the Japanese attack. This conclusion proved completely contrary to the findings of both the Army Pearl Harbor Board and the Naval Court of Inquiry four years later, and contrary to the joint congressional committee findings five years later.

Fifty-nine years later, Congress passed a law trying to stop perpetuation of the myth. Both officers, Kimmel and Short, deserve posthumous advancement in rank.

THOMAS K. KIMMEL, JR., is the grandson of Admiral Husband E. Kimmel. A graduate of the U.S. Naval Academy, he is a lawyer and former FBI agent and consultant.

Justice Was Served
by Frederic L. Borch III

An increasingly loud chorus of politicians, retired naval officers, commentators, historians, and friends have joined the Kimmel and Short families in demanding that Admiral Husband E. Kimmel and General Walter C. Short be posthumously advanced to the four-star and three-star ranks they held on December 7, 1941. Only this official action, they cry, will eradicate the stain that has tarnished their honor and reputations—a stain that resulted when civilian and military leaders in Washington unjustly held them responsible for the greatest single defeat ever suffered by American naval forces.

Those in favor of promoting Kimmel and Short advance a two-part justification. First, they claim that the two commanders were punished in the aftermath of the Japanese attack on Pearl Harbor—this punishment taking the form of a forced retirement at two-star rank. Second, they argue that the punishment was unfair and unjust because Kimmel and Short did the best they could in defending Hawaii. In fact, claim the Kimmel-Short "defense team," civilian and military leaders in Washington were to blame for the inadequate defense of Oahu because these high-level officials failed to provide the men and materiel necessary to mount a successful defense of Hawaii. More important, they adamantly insist that leaders in Washington withheld highly secret and valuable intelligence from Kimmel and Short—information that would have caused the two commanders to anticipate and successfully defend against the Japanese surprise attack. Since this means that culpability rests with Washington rather than Hawaii, it follows that Kimmel and Short were falsely blamed for the disaster, and this injustice will only be remedied by restoring their higher ranks.

A close look at the historical record, however, shows that those who would absolve Kimmel and Short of responsibility are simply wrong. Their claims to the contrary, posthumous promotion for either man is not warranted for at least four reasons.

First, neither Kimmel nor Short were punished in the aftermath of the Pearl Harbor attack. Consequently, it is wrong to continue to claim that a posthumous advancement in rank is now needed to "undo" a punishment.

Second, Admiral Kimmel and General Short did not do their best. Knowing that war with Japan was imminent and that their commands might be targeted, both men failed to make preparations to defend against such an attack.

Third, Washington was not to blame for the magnitude of the disaster on December 7, 1941. The War and Navy Departments did not withhold intelligence that would have warned Kimmel and Short of an impending Japanese attack—for no such intelligence existed. No U.S. official

knew that Japanese aircraft would attack Oahu on December 7. For Kimmel and Short's defenders to claim otherwise is simply false—and a transparent attempt to shift blame to others.

Finally, as the senior sea and land commanders, Kimmel and Short were responsible for everything that did or did not happen in their commands. This so-called principle of command responsibility is the fourth reason that posthumous promotion is inappropriate.

On December 9, Secretary of the Navy Frank Knox arrived in Pearl Harbor. He was there not only to find out what had happened, but also to try to understand why. After personally interviewing Kimmel, Short, and their staffs, and seeing firsthand the death and destruction wrought by the Japanese, Knox concluded that the success of the enemy attack "was due to a lack of a state of readiness." According to Knox, both Kimmel and Short admitted to him that they did not expect an aerial attack, "and had taken no adequate measures to meet one if it came." Knox delivered his final report to President Roosevelt on December 14. Two days later, after consulting with the president, Knox and his army counterpart, Secretary of War Stimson, relieved Kimmel and Short of their commands. Under the law of the time, all four- and three-star rank was temporary; Admiral Kimmel and Lt. Gen. Short had permanent grades of rear admiral and major general, respectively. Consequently, when relieved of their Hawaiian commands, they automatically reverted to their two-star grades.

On December 18, 1941, President Roosevelt established a five-member commission, headed by Supreme Court Justice Owen J. Roberts, to determine whether "any derelictions or errors of judgment on the part of United States Army or Navy personnel contributed to such successes as were achieved by the enemy." The Roberts Com-

mission was further directed to establish who was responsible for any derelictions or errors. After interviewing 127 witnesses and examining a variety of documents, the commission concluded that Kimmel and Short, knowing that hostilities with Japan were imminent, were derelict in their duties in failing "to consult and confer" with each other in preparing their defense of Oahu.

Given the conclusions announced in the Knox and Roberts reports, Kimmel and Short soon realized that new assignments, commensurate with their former positions in Hawaii, were not going to be given to them. Short then decided to submit his retirement papers, and although he hoped his application to retire would be rejected, it was not. When Admiral Kimmel learned that Short had requested retirement, he took this as a signal that he should do so as well. The result was that Maj. Gen. Short retired on February 28, 1942, and Rear Adm. Kimmel retired on March 1, 1942. Neither man was forced into retirement— and there is no evidence to support claims to the contrary. Additionally, both men retired without having been charged with any criminal offense (dereliction of duty was *not* a court-martial offense in 1941).

While there was some talk of court-martial, both the army and navy decided that criminal trials were inappropriate. The army judge advocate general, for example, concluded that Short's mistakes at Pearl Harbor "were honest ones, not the result of conscious fault and, having in mind all the circumstances, do not constitute a criminal neglect of duty." Finally, neither Kimmel nor Short was ever administratively censured. They were never officially reprimanded. They left active duty with their official records unblemished and retired in 1942 at the highest possible rank and pay grade.

Only in 1947, as a reward to those who served in World War II, did Congress decide to permit those who had served in

three-, four-, and five-star grades to retire with those extra stars. At the time, army and navy leaders could have requested that Kimmel and Short be advanced to their higher ranks. The service secretaries, however, decided that their performance on December 7, 1941, did not merit an advancement in rank. While this meant that Kimmel and Short were the only two flag officers not recommended for promotion to their highest wartime ranks, their performance in one of the greatest defeats suffered by American armed forces was a good reason to treat them differently.

When the secretaries of the navy and the army declined to recommend Kimmel and Short for promotion in 1947, this was not a punishment. On the contrary, it was simply a decision to withhold the privilege of high rank. In sum, Kimmel and Short were not punished in the aftermath of the death and destruction at Pearl Harbor, and promoting them today is not needed to undo or rectify an unjust or unfair punishment.

Admiral Kimmel and General Short simply did not do their best while in command in Hawaii, and their substandard performance is the best reason to refuse to promote them. It is significant that virtually every investigation into the events of December 7, 1941, concluded that Kimmel and Short failed to adequately defend their forces.

From 1941 to '46, there were nine separate Pearl Harbor investigations. All but one—a purely naval inquiry whose conclusions were rejected by Admiral Ernest King, then the chief of Naval Operations— determined that the two senior commanders were either derelict in their duties or at least made errors in judgment.

Thus the first investigation, conducted by Secretary of the Navy Knox from December 9 to 14, 1941, concluded that the "Japanese air attack…was a complete surprise" because both Kimmel and Short did not believe an attack likely and consequently were unprepared to meet it. Simi-

larly, the second investigation, conducted by a five-member commission headed by Justice Roberts in late December 1941 and early January '42, reached an identical conclusion: Kimmel and Short were derelict in their duties to defend Oahu. The 1946 investigation conducted by a joint committee of Congress—which heard testimony from hundreds of witnesses, including Admiral Kimmel and General Short, and examined thousands of pages of documentary evidence—concluded that the two commanders made "errors of judgment" in preparing to defend Hawaii from attack. Finally, the most recent official investigation, conducted by the Department of Defense in 1996—an investigation intentionally done outside the Departments of the Army and Navy to ensure that there would be no prejudice or preconceived ideas about what happened at Pearl Harbor— reached the same conclusion: Kimmel and Short committed "errors of judgment." Consequently, they are responsible, in part, for the magnitude of the losses suffered by U.S. forces on December 7.

What were these errors in judgment? First, Kimmel failed to employ torpedo netting in and around Pearl Harbor—nets that could have stopped the Japanese torpedoes that hit *Utah*, *Oklahoma*, *Nevada*, *West Virginia*, *California* and other navy vessels. Although his superiors had warned Kimmel that the U.S. fleet was at risk from air-dropped torpedoes, Kimmel concluded that the waters at Pearl were shallow enough to disregard that danger.

Second, neither Kimmel nor Short employed barrage balloons in the airspace over Pearl Harbor—aerial obstacles that could have disrupted the air approaches of enemy attackers. Again, although his superiors in Washington had recommended such a defensive device to Short, it was rejected as impracticable.

Third, Short failed to use his radar assets appropriately. While radio detecting

and ranging devices were primitive, Short and his staff knew that the British had used radar in winning the Battle of Britain in 1940. Yet, as Short testified in 1946, he considered radar to be for "training" only. These Kimmel-Short missteps, however, pale in significance when compared with two other errors in judgment: Kimmel's failure to do any reconnaissance and a general failure on the part of both Kimmel and Short to integrate—or even coordinate— their defense of the islands.

Although General Short was primarily responsible for the defense of the Hawaiian Islands, Kimmel and Short agreed between themselves that the navy would perform the long-range reconnaissance critical to detecting the approach of an enemy. Short subsequently assumed that the navy was fulfilling its responsibilities. Kimmel, however, would conclude that he did not have enough aircraft to do a complete, 360-degree reconnaissance. Believing that anything less than such a lookout was not worth the effort, Kimmel elected to do no reconnaissance. That was a grievous error in judgment, for it meant that there was no real chance to detect the arrival of 353 Japanese aircraft that Sunday morning. Kimmel failed to understand that he did have sufficient aircraft to do some reconnaissance. He certainly could have combined his thirty-six patrol bombers with Short's twelve B-17s and thirty-two B-18s to do some long-range patrolling. Additionally, Kimmel had three aircraft carriers, nine battleships, twelve heavy cruisers, nine light cruisers, and fifty-three destroyers. These eighty-six ships could have been used, in conjunction with aircraft, to conduct long-range scouting.

For Kimmel, however, it was an all-or-nothing proposition, and he had chosen nothing. Unfortunately for Kimmel's sailors and marines, and Short's soldiers, this lack of reconnaissance virtually ensured that there would be no warning of an approaching attacker. While there is no

Smoke, bursts of anti-aircraft fire, and attacking Japanese aircraft fill the sky, in John Hamilton's Battleship Row—Pearl Harbor. *Sixty years after the "day of infamy," lingering questions of U.S. command responsibility may have relevance to modern tragedies.*

way to know whether a different choice, such as partial reconnaissance focusing on likely avenues of approach to the west and north, might have discovered the Japanese armada, Kimmel's decision was a critical reason for the huge losses of life and materiel suffered on December 7.

Finally, Kimmel and Short also failed to integrate—or even coordinate—their command-and-control structure. This lack of a unified defense effort was a serious error in judgment. It meant, for example, that Short believed the navy was conducting long-range reconnaissance even though Kimmel had elected to do none. It meant that Kimmel did not know that the army's greatest fear was sabotage and that, as a result, the army had its ammunition under lock and key. Nor did Kimmel know that Short's aircraft were lined up neatly in rows so that it was difficult for them to get quickly airborne.

This lack of coordination meant that the army never knew that the destroyer USS *Ward* had been in a fight with an enemy submarine at 6:40 A.M. Of course, Kimmel never heard about the sinking of the submarine either, because his own command-and-control system was so deficient that it prevented valuable information from reaching him and other senior navy leaders in Hawaii. Had Kimmel instilled a sense of urgency and alertness in his command, there is no reason that he and Short could not have learned of *Ward's* engagement at least an hour before the Japanese planes appeared at 7:55 A.M.

Similarly, an integrated or coordinated defense might have meant that a report

that two young radar operators had detected a large aircraft formation at 7:02 would have been taken more seriously. Certainly this radar sighting, when combined with *Ward's* sinking of an enemy submarine, would likely have led an integrated or coordinated command structure to recognize that there was a clear and real danger to American forces in Hawaii. Stated differently, a unified or coordinated defense, instilled with a sense of urgency, would most probably have given Kimmel and Short the very tactical warning that they needed to mitigate the effect of the Japanese onslaught.

How could Kimmel and Short have been so unready? How could they have made such errors in judgment? To a great extent, their unpreparedness resulted from two factors. One was simply an inability to appreciate how technology—particularly air power—had altered warfare. Both Kimmel and Short stated publicly in the summer of 1941 that an aerial attack on Hawaii was "a possibility" (Kimmel) and "not... improbable" (Short). Both men had received a written "War Warning" from Washington on November 27, in which they were informed not only that war with Japan was likely, but that "an aggressive move" was expected "within the next few days." While both commanders did believe that war with Japan was coming, neither Kimmel nor Short understood that war might mean an attack against the U.S. Pacific Fleet while in port at Pearl Harbor. As a result, Short prepared a defense against sabotage, while Kimmel prepared for war on the high seas.

This shortsightedness—the failure to envisage that an attack on their commands was possible—infected their subordinates with a "peacetime-in-Hawaii" mentality. Thus, Kimmel's sailors and marines trained hard during the week, but on weekends the U.S. fleet was tied up neatly at its moorings, with hatches open, boilers cold, and sailors on liberty. The Japanese knew this, and they planned their attack for Sunday morning precisely because they anticipated that Kimmel would have the fleet in port and unready.

This peacetime attitude meant that when USS *Ward* sank an enemy submarine at the entrance to Pearl Harbor and quickly reported the fight to the naval district watch officer, Kimmel's subordinates were still debating its significance when the first Japanese bombs fell seventy-five minutes later. It was no better in Short's command. Consequently, after mobile radar sites on northern Oahu spotted a large formation of incoming aircraft at 7:02 A.M. and relayed that information to the army watch officer at Fort Shafter, that officer ignored the report because he thought the radar had identified a group of U.S. B-17s flying in from California. Of course, the radar in fact had picked up the attacking Japanese air formations.

Kimmel's own words perhaps best explain why American forces were caught so unready and unprepared. In an interview with the famous correspondent Joseph Harsch on December 6, Harsch asked Kimmel if he thought the Japanese might attack Hawaii. Replied Kimmel: "I don't think they'd be such damned fools." If the senior American naval commander in Hawaii had this view, his subordinates were unlikely to think otherwise. No doubt this explains why Kimmel thought he could schedule a golf game for the morning of December 7, which he would have played had the Japanese not started dropping their bombs at 7:55 A.M.

Those seeking exoneration for Kimmel and Short claim that Washington also withheld much-needed men and materiel from the two commanders—resources required to mount a successful defense. Thus, for example, they claim that a lack of aircraft excuses Kimmel's failure to conduct long-range reconnaissance. The reality, however, is that both Admiral Kimmel and General Short had adequate resources at their disposal. No commander ever gets everything he wants; there are always competing demands for men and materiel. At the time, with U.S. naval forces fighting an undeclared war with U-boats in the Battle of the Atlantic, Kimmel could not be given everything that he requested. But he had eighty-six ships in his command, and he and Short had at least eighty aircraft capable of long-range reconnaissance. They had more than adequate resources to defend their commands.

The more serious allegation is that civilian and military leaders in Washington—President Franklin D. Roosevelt, Army Chief of Staff General George C. Marshall, and Chief of Naval Operations Harold R. Stark—withheld valuable information from Admiral Kimmel and General Short. This information, obtained from deciphered Japanese messages, is supposed to have revealed that the Japanese intended to attack Hawaii on December 7. The reality, however, is that this information simply did not exist. No one in the U.S. government knew that the Japanese carriers were heading for Hawaiian waters. No American official—in Washington or anywhere else—knew that an attack on Oahu would occur on December 7.

While it is true that the U.S. Navy had broken, and was regularly deciphering and reading, Japanese diplomatic codes, the information that passed between Tokyo and its embassies and consulates did not contain details of any impending Japanese attack. On the contrary, while the diplomatic messages were exceedingly valuable as an indicator of Japanese strategic intentions, these transmissions did not contain the type of intelligence that might have been gleaned from decoded military and naval radio traffic.

American intelligence, however, had not broken the Japanese military codes—nor had anyone else. Despite their best efforts, American and British code-breakers were able to read Japanese military traffic to only "a very small degree." This is an important distinction, for it means that Magic—the name given by U.S. intelligence to the deciphered diplomatic messages—never revealed the particulars of any Japanese military operations. Most important, Magic never revealed that an attack on Pearl Harbor was imminent.

In any event, even if U.S. intelligence had broken the Japanese military and naval codes, it would have made no difference because there simply never was any radio traffic between Japanese forces that indicated that an attack on Hawaii had been planned or was being executed. And the Japanese made sure that no such messages could be intercepted, since the imperial carriers steaming from Japan toward Hawaii maintained complete radio silence after leaving their home waters on November 26. In short, the claim that Kimmel and Short were deprived of valuable intelligence that might have alerted them of an impending attack is simply false, and an attempt to shift blame from where it belongs.

Finally, the principle of command responsibility makes it both fair and equitable for Kimmel and Short to bear some measure of responsibility for what happened at Pearl Harbor. Officers in command, at all levels and in all branches of the service, are responsible for everything that their units do, or fail to do. In the navy, this means that the skipper of a frigate is responsible for damage to his ship if it runs aground, even though a sub-

ordinate's navigational error may be the actual cause of the mishap. For Kimmel and Short, this meant that they were responsible for the safety and security of all U.S. forces in Hawaii.

Knowing that Japan was already at war in Asia, and having been warned that hostilities with enemy forces were imminent, Kimmel and Short were required to use all the resources at their disposal to prepare for battle with Japan—and prepare to defend against any possible attack from that enemy. While it is true that an attack on Oahu seemed highly unlikely, their jobs were to anticipate the unexpected. This they failed to do, and this failure was the proximate cause of the terribly disproportionate losses suffered by America during that December 7 attack. It follows that, as the most senior commanders in Hawaii, they bear command responsibility for the disaster at Pearl Harbor.

In conclusion, Kimmel and Short do not merit posthumous advancement to four-star and three-star rank. They failed to demonstrate the superior judgment expected of commanders of their grade and experience, for they made bad choices in the days, weeks, and months preceding the Japanese surprise attack. While it appears that their errors in judgment did not justify criminal proceedings against them, their mistakes nevertheless cost America much loss of life. In the words of Admiral Trost, who served as chief of Naval Operations during the late 1980s, "there is a vast difference between a degree of fault which does not warrant a punitive action and a level of performance which would warrant bestowal of a privilege." As Kimmel and Short were responsible at Pearl Harbor, and as posthumous advancement would bestow a privilege upon them, it is wrong to do so.

FREDERIC L. BORCH III is a colonel in the Judge Advocate General's Corps.

HENRY VIII'S
UNLIKELY NAVAL HERO

King Henry flouted protocol when he named one of his favorites to command the newly expanded English fleet. Although plagued by defeats and setbacks, Lord Admiral Edward Howard nevertheless became England's first naval hero.

by Robert L. Swain

At age twenty-two, Henry VIII was three years into his reign and fired by the belief that England shared his appetite for the glory and spoils of war. As it developed, he guessed right, for in January 1512 the usually tight-fisted members of Parliament granted him funds for a season of warfare against their traditional enemy, France. Tales of Henry V's great victory at Agincourt, almost a century before, were recalled for the enjoyment of a new generation of Englishmen.

Eager to plan his coming invasion properly, Henry huddled with his principal adviser, Thomas Wolsey, in the chilly royal palace at Greenwich. There, without the interference of others, they discussed who could best command the country's eighteen-ship fleet (with more on the way). The two of them agreed the choice should be someone able to bring the recently expanded fleet rapidly to fighting readiness, clear the English Channel of enemy ships, and lead a series of harassing raids along the French coast from Brest to Calais. Success in these endeavors would ensure safe passage of troops south to assist Henry's father-in-law, King Ferdinand II of Aragon, in a joint Anglo-Spanish attack on Aquitaine, which France had recovered by the end of the Hundred Years' War in 1453.

One of the first English ships built expressly for warfare, Mary Rose boasted more than two hundred guns and served as the flagship of Lord Admiral Edward Howard's fleet (Pepys Library, Magdalene College, Cambridge).

Henry and Wolsey debated a number of candidates, with Henry stating a clear preference for one of his hunting companions: Lord Edward Howard, the thirty-seven-year-old bachelor son of the lord treasurer and earl of Surrey, Thomas Howard I. While Lord Edward had command experience, choosing him to be lord admiral presented a difficulty. It meant overlooking Edward's older brother, Lord Thomas Howard II, who had played the leading role, between the brothers, in the recent pursuit and capture at sea of James Barton, Scotland's lord admiral.

Henry had grown up with Thomas and Edward Howard as older-brother figures and had come to admire the more dashing Edward over Thomas, who lacked his younger brother's spontaneity and was too dour for Henry. Going with his personal

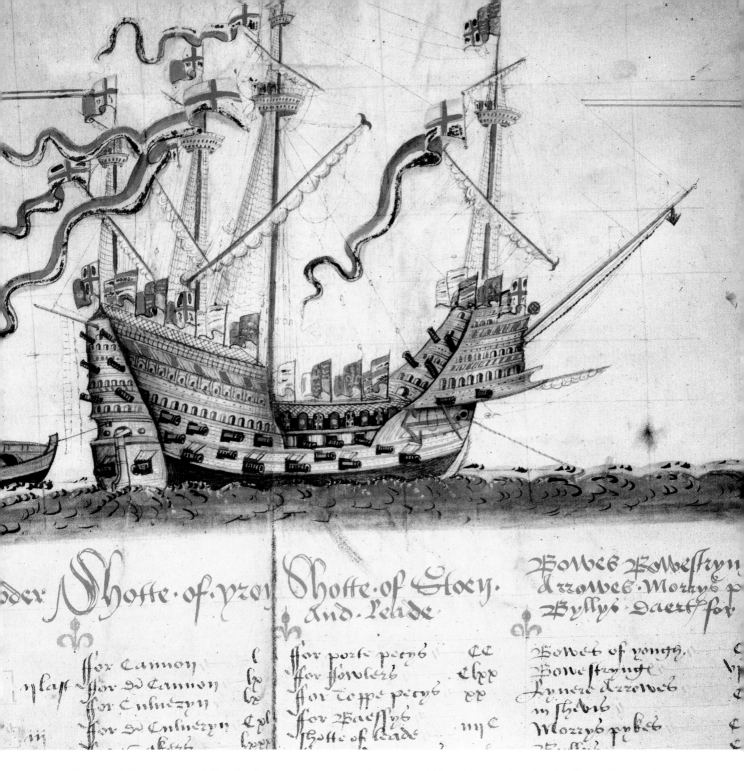

favorite also meant that Henry would break a long-standing tradition that called for first sons to be picked ahead of younger brothers for high office or field command. But Henry had been a neglected younger brother himself, and this may have represented an opportunity to even the score for second sons.

As could have been anticipated (and probably was by Wolsey), the choice of Edward Howard for lord admiral raised a stink among the older nobility. This group was well aware of Edward's bachelor lifestyle and knew that he had displeased his father by siring illegitimate children. They could empathize also with Surrey's dismay over tradition turned upside down for the benefit of an undisciplined younger son, particularly if commoner Wolsey had a hand in it. None of this, however, appeared

to concern Edward Howard, and as for Henry, he was determined to prevail—and so did he.

Outwardly indifferent to protocol or to anyone's disappointment, Henry allowed Wolsey to announce that the new lord admiral was to have a generous allotment of three thousand men under his overall command. Further, Edward Howard's flagship, *Mary Rose*, was to have a complement of seven hundred men, double the normal crew. The ship would be armed with brass muzzleloading guns, each weighing about three thousand pounds. The fleet was to be resupplied every three months, another display of generous support.

The six-hundred-ton, four-decked *Mary Rose* was Henry's pride. The largest ship in the royal fleet, she carried four masts,

120 oars, and more than two hundred guns, some of which were nearly twelve feet long. Henry had ordered *Mary Rose* (named for his favorite sister) to be built just after his coronation, and he had followed the ship's design and construction with close interest. Although the king's council of older men found it hard to keep him focused, developing the navy was a duty the glory-minded Henry enjoyed fully.

Edward Howard joined *Mary Rose* at Plymouth, where she was being outfitted for the coming campaign. Items consigned to the ship included 300 pikes, 300 bills, 220 sets of armor, 350 six-foot-long yew bows, 700 bowstrings, and 700 sheaves of armor-piercing arrows. Also loaded aboard the flagship was a large quantity of darts and stones. The men hauled the darts aloft to the tops and stacked the various-sized shot by the guns. In this instance, the shot included iron for smashing hulls, stone for splintering masts, and crossbar shot for shredding riggings. Finally, there was hollow shot filled with lead pellets to spread like hail against enemy personnel in the event of a close encounter with an enemy ship.

By royal commission, Edward Howard was to be served by a staff of thirty-one, including a "treasurer of the army by sea." Henry went further by granting his admiral the privilege of having twenty personal servants on board and permission to enlist two of his brothers-in-law to serve as ship captains. These considerations continued to magnify the slight felt by Surrey and his oldest son, Thomas, who had been consigned to a meaningless land assignment.

Edward Howard, elated with his appointment, seemed oblivious to his family's embarrassment. During his youth, his father had been absent for years, first in the Tower of London for being on the wrong side at the Battle of Bosworth Field during the War of the Roses, and then posted to the Scottish border for another ten years. Edward's older brother had been a companion at court and in jousting with Henry, but they were of strikingly different temperaments and were not close.

Impatient to be underway with his command, Edward Howard sailed *Mary Rose* from Plymouth in late February 1512 to join the assembled fleet anchored off the royal docks at Southampton. There, under persistently gray skies, the new lord admiral quickly expressed dismay over delays in supplying the fleet. Unable to contain himself, he wrote Henry directly, saying, "Sir, for God's sake haste your council to send me down our victuals, for if we shall lie long, the common voice will run that we lie and keep in the Downs, and do no good but spend money." This last comment was a thinly disguised gibe at his father, who was known to be critical of Wolsey's spending, which was often independent of Surrey's approval at treasury.

As expected, Edward Howard's father was annoyed by his son's suggestion of council inactivity, but Wolsey ignored Surrey and saw to it that Edward was promptly supplied. Southampton took on a busy air. Food and beer were acquired at considerable cost and transported to the docksides. Finally ready, and with favorable winds, the lord admiral was underway by mid-March. His fleet was the first in the English Channel when war was shortly thereafter declared against France.

Henry VIII displayed his commitment to England's navy in 1509, the year he was coronated, when he laid down Mary Rose *in Portsmouth's shipyard. To command the new fleet, however, he violated tradition by choosing Edward Howard instead of Edward's older brother, Lord Thomas Howard II.*

Mary Rose had led the way with her greater speed, but a difficult passage in Dover Straits had tested the entire fleet. Changing winds forced every ship to constantly tack, and Howard thought it fortunate that all came through safely. Although the crews were fairly exhausted by the effort, the lord admiral and his captains kept the sense of excitement alive for everyone. Gaining more experience by the day, Howard aggressively pursued Channel shipping and swept it clear by early June. It mattered not to him whether they encountered French ships, Flemish fishing boats, or Spanish merchantmen. The English fleet harassed them all during its first ten weeks at sea.

Asked by Henry to "send word how every ship did sail," Howard faithfully wrote about each ship under his command on his return for supplies. He commented, "the *Sovereign*, after the *Mary Rose*, is the noblest ship of sail at this hour in Christendom." *Sovereign*, which dated from Henry VII's time, carried 141 guns, almost sixty less than *Mary Rose*, and had been previously used to transport goods from the Mediterranean. The lord admiral continued to praise *Sovereign*, observing that "a ship of a hundred tons will not sooner come about than she." Howard added that *Nicholas*, *Leonard of Dartmouth*, *George*, *Harry of Hampton*, and *Anne* were all fine ships, but that *Catherine* was "over laden with ordnance." This would have

An outgoing bachelor who fathered several children, Lord Admiral Howard, depicted in his final battle, was a longtime favorite of King Henry's. But Howard's impulsiveness eventually cost him his life (Peter Newark's Military Pictures).

was a violent collision, breaking a huge hole in the bottom of the ship and causing her to sink within minutes.

Given the point of honor among English seamen not to learn to swim lest they be thought to lack faith in their ship's ability to return safely to port, the loss was nearly total, as the crew perished after struggling with the waves. Horrified and dispirited by the loss, Howard signaled the other ships to break off the intended assault and ordered the fleet to return to Plymouth for reprovisioning.

Howard was embarrassed by the loss of a ship, and also concerned for the credibility of his command. He nervously sent word to Henry that *Mary Rose* was "your good ship, the flower of all ships that ever sailed" and worthy of being tested in battle. Again, he had only one negative comment: The three-hundred-ton *Christ* "was one of the worse that day."

Meanwhile, Henry was anxious to see the fleet himself upon its return to Plymouth. He gathered an escort at Windsor and promptly made the long journey there to visit with his lord admiral and captains of the returning ships. Once in Plymouth, Henry forgot the recent loss as he took in his fleet standing at anchor, colorful banners fluttering from every mast. It was an impressive sight for everyone in the harbor and crowding along the dockside, and helped to reinforce the belief that the young king was the richest monarch in Europe.

Dressed in a splendid naval uniform for the occasion, Henry greeted Howard warmly, as sailors piped him aboard the flagship. There was no mention of the ship and crew lost off Brest Harbor. Instead, Henry offered to host a banquet onboard *Mary Rose* before the fleet sailed again to resume attacks on the French coast. Accordingly, captains from the fleet were rowed over to *Mary Rose* to accept the king's hospitality. It was all very jovial, as Henry played the noble knight before his men.

During the banquet, an exuberant Edward Howard suggested to Henry that he sail with them to inspire a naval victory. Slightly drunk, and much taken with the idea, Henry said yes. However, when several members of his council along on the trip overheard this, they quickly objected and asked Henry to reconsider, pointing out that an English monarch had never sailed into battle with a fleet before. No one seemed to recall that Edward III had commanded the fleet at the 1340 naval Battle of Sluys, but that was long ago. More to the point, Henry was told he must not expose himself to such danger, since he had no direct heir yet. This was sufficient to end the discussion.

made her top-heavy and difficult to handle in the Channel. Budding naval enthusiast Henry was delighted with the lord admiral's assessments, and even Wolsey was reassured by the fleet's readiness for war against France.

The French had learned of England's mobilization before the declaration of war and were not surprised to sight Howard's fleet when it cruised menacingly along their coast, heading toward Brest. Despite this warning, France's ability to defend its west coast was limited by its concurrent military involvement in northern Italy. Aware of this distraction, Howard had planned to assault Brest, near the western tip of Brittany, to prevent the French from using it as a base for their dreaded Mediterranean galley fleet should it be transferred northward.

Pressing ahead with his plan in the summer of 1512, Howard approached Brest under a bright sun, which created an extraordinary glare on the waters ahead. Not fully appreciating the danger this presented to navigation, the intrepid lord admiral was dismayed to see one of his ships running up on a blind rock. It

Once back in London, the full council succeeded in persuading the impulsive Henry that he was more valuable to the coming enterprise against France on land with an army. The idea of the sovereign sailing anywhere with the fleet was forgotten, to everyone's relief. Edward Howard's urging such a choice on the king, who probably had second thoughts himself, undoubtedly angered the increasingly irascible Surrey.

Oblivious to his father's reaction, Edward Howard continued to busy himself at Southampton, while Wolsey worked diligently to support the fleet's refitting. Foodstuffs, beer, munitions, and related gear were assembled and sent to the fleet with such dispatch that Howard had his ships off Brest again within days of the final loading. This time he anticipated the glare of the sun, kept the fleet well free of the rocks, and managed to put several detachments of men ashore. Their orders were to raid the surrounding countryside as a prelude to a combined land and sea assault on the French port.

In an effort to shield the landing from any seaborne surprise, Howard ordered one of his captains, Anthony Ughtred, to hold his ship, *Mary James*, well offshore. Ughtred was disappointed to miss the action, but he reluctantly obliged the lord admiral. The precaution paid off when, on August 10, the captain sighted a French warship approaching two leagues off. He immediately sailed to engage the newcomer, *La Cordelière*, captained by corsair Hervé de Portznoguer.

As the ships closed on each other in a good breeze, the aggressive Ughtred held to a collision course under full sail, with bowmen aloft in the fighting tops and cannons at ready in the open ports. Moving faster than the one-thousand-ton *La Cordelière*, the lighter *Mary James* rammed the French ship, which was packed with eight hundred men-at-arms, four hundred crossbowmen, and fifty gunners. The collision's force splintered a portion of *La Cordelière*'s side, turning her bow into the wind and causing her sails to noisily spill their wind.

Mary James and *La Cordelière* swung on each other's beam amid shouts and curses, while English bowmen fired down on the enemy deck. Above the din, Ughtred bellowed orders to his gunners to fire point-blank into *La Cordelière*. They lit the fuses, and the English cannons belched eighteen-pound shot in a deafening roar, then violently recoiled. Acrid powder smoke swirled over the ships, while cries of the wounded could be heard from the enemy vessel. Surviving French gunners managed to respond in kind, but Ughtred's men got off another round before the guns on both ships fell largely silent. The ships drifted in a haze of smoke.

The damage to both vessels was extensive, and men lay wounded and dying on each. Barely noticed by the French, two other English ships were bearing down to attack *La Cordelière* from the other side. The first was the one-thousand-ton *Regent*,

French sailors abandon ship as La Cordelière *erupts in flames during her August 10, 1512, battle with Howard's fleet. The vessel's captain, Hervé de Portznoguer, jumped or fell overboard in full armor and sank straight to the bottom.*

Above the din, Ughtred bellowed orders to his gunners to fire point-blank into *La Cordelière*.

with seven hundred men aboard, under the joint command of Howard's brothers-in-law, Thomas Knevet and John Carew. The second vessel was the slightly smaller *Sovereign*, with 141 guns, commanded by Charles Brandon, a boon companion of the lord admiral's and the king's.

Regent looked impressive, with her four masts and the main carrying a topgallant as well. She had 225 guns in all, which were designed to be effective in sweeping an enemy ship's decks and rigging. This new assault might have been the *coup de grâce* for the French ship, but a well-placed shot from the heavily damaged *La Cordelière* shattered the approaching *Sovereign*'s main mast. This left Brandon with little choice but to break off his attack.

Although *Sovereign* was out of the fight, *Regent* continued to close on *La Cordelière*. Archers on the English ship loosed a deadly hail of arrows on the enemy, killing and wounding even more Frenchmen. The survivors of this assault sought cover as best they could, while men on *Regent* grappled her to the French ship's side. Once she was secured, several hundred English soldiers clambered onto *La Cordelière*. Victory for *Regent* now seemed within easy grasp, but misfortune intervened when Knevet was cut in half by one of the last cannon shots fired from the French ship as he was shouting commands to the boarding party.

At first unnoticed, fires broke out on both *La Cordelière* and *Regent*, but then flames began to race up the rigging of the French ship and consume her sails. In the excitement, other fires belowdecks on both ships found their way unimpeded to the powder magazines. Thunderous explosions then rocked both ships, blowing hundreds of men into the air. Giant flames roared out from gunports, as Portznoguer, in full armor, jumped or fell overboard and vanished beneath the waves.

Regent and *La Cordelière* seemed to disappear in gun smoke and raging flames. Terrified survivors on both ships screamed and cursed as they struggled to escape the fires burning out of control by throwing themselves into the sea. Desperate, Ughtred attempted to maneuver *Mary James* away from the inferno. Over on *Regent*, Howard's other brother-in-law, co-captain Carew, perished in the flames. All three captains on the cruelly tethered ships had lost their lives.

The burning hulks drifted with the wind and current, no longer capable of guided action. Brandon, on *Sovereign*, ordered boats lowered to pick up survivors. On *La Cordelière*, only twenty sailors and soldiers remained alive, while less than one-fifth of *Regent*'s crew of seven hundred had survived. A later report gave the number of French survivors as only six, suggesting that some of the twenty ultimately died of burns.

Howard, overcome with frustration, had to watch the unprecedented disaster from a distance. Stunned by the loss of so many men and another of his ships, the lord admiral was compelled to recall his landing parties and pull away from Brest. But he was reluctant to withdraw completely and held the fleet several miles off the port for the next two days. On the second day he sent several new raiding parties ashore to sack what they could and to take prisoners, almost as compensation for the dreadful

loss of *Regent*. Finally setting sail for England, the sorrowful lord admiral began his report to Henry and Wolsey, pledging to avenge the loss of Knevet and Carew.

In London, Wolsey shared the lord admiral's report with Bishop Fox, his closest colleague on the king's council. As he did so, Wolsey cautioned the bishop to "keep this tidings secret to yourself, for there is no living man knoweth the same here but only the king and I." In his view, the public should not know about the loss of *Regent* until there was some encouraging news to balance the bad. As it was, the crown easily managed to camouflage the loss in that age of no newspapers, television, radio, or question periods in the House of Commons.

The lord admiral returned home to disband the men of the fleet until the coming season. It was to be a difficult winter for the grieving Edward Howard, estranged from his family and finding little opportunity to spend time with the king, although nothing was said about the disaster off Brest. A greater angst for Henry was with the dismal failure of the expedition to support his father-in-law in Aquitaine. As for the loss of *Regent*, he considered that a terrible accident and agreed with Wolsey to say nothing publicly.

All during the winter, Howard obsessed at home over the importance of avenging the deaths of Knevet and Carew and making it possible for Henry to announce a worthy victory over the French in the coming campaign season. Still on edge in late March, the lord admiral was cheered to learn through informers that the French fleet recently assembled at Brest intended to come out and contest his mastery of the English Channel that spring.

Howard was eager to take up the challenge and boasted to Wolsey that if he could recall his crews and be underway shortly, his fleet could dispense with the French in no more than five or six days. This optimism about confronting the reawakened French helped Wolsey to raise enough money to permit the hiring and outfitting of seven more warships, which would bring the fleet to more than fifty ships.

After his crews were reassembed, Howard's intentions were compromised by an unexpected shortage of beer and biscuits. Concerned aides urged him to delay his departure, pointing out that no English army fought without its beer, but Howard

seemed not to hear and ordered the fleet to sail without waiting for the victuals. He could not waste any time if he hoped to find the French fleet still in the harbor at Brest.

Despite protests and misgivings, Howard had the fleet off Brest within weeks. Once within sight of their destination, he and his officers on *Mary Rose* were elated to see twenty-two French ships anchored there. It was early afternoon, and the French crews were still celebrating a feast day. Unaware of the approaching English, the lieutenant general of the fleet, René de Clermont, was entertaining three hundred local dignitaries and their wives aboard his flagship, *Grande Luise,* which was nearly twice the size of *Mary Rose*. When the French lookouts finally sighted the English fleet, the French admiral immediately ordered *Grande Luise*'s anchor hauled in and sails set. His intent was to reach the outer bay quickly enough to interrupt any bombardment by the enemy.

were ready in their armor, with archers posted in the lower rigging and along the sides of the main deck. Once in range, gunners on *Mary Rose* were ordered to fire on the larger *Grande Luise*, and they did so with remarkable and deadly accuracy. The English cannonade wounded or killed an extraordinary number on the French flagship and shattered her main mast. Without recourse, the French admiral watched his crippled ship drift toward the shore, where she luckily gained the protection of the shore batteries, making further pursuit by Howard on *Mary Rose* too risky. Word was sent to Henry that the French fleet was bottled up in Brest Harbor.

The English cruised off Brest for the next two days without serious challenge, although they overtook and captured several French ships that tested the blockade. Howard took eight hundred Frenchmen prisoner in the process, but Henry's response to the earlier message only contained the question: "Why is the French fleet only bottled up and not yet destroyed?" Stung by Henry's inquiry, Howard impulsively landed men on the French coast and sent raiding parties toward Brest. Meanwhile, it was discovered that the French Mediterranean fleet of galleys, with its much-feared firepower, had appeared on the horizon.

It proved a remarkable turn of events—the combined French fleets now outnumbered Howard's force. To make matters worse, the English were low on supplies, and Howard also realized he had too few troops and artillery ashore to take Brest by land. The strain was beginning to show among his officers, as arguments erupted over what to do. Only the appearance of a supply ship that had managed to slip by the French Mediterranean fleet interrupted the dissension.

Lord Admiral Howard saw what was happening and, in the disappearing daylight, ordered his fleet to drop anchor and wait for the dawn before going into action. This allowed the French admiral, barely underway, to come about and anchor as well. It also gave him the opportunity to ferry his now thoroughly fatigued guests to safe haven ashore, while several other French ships joined *Grande Luise* on station.

When the sun came up the following morning, the French realized how outnumbered they were. Clermont could see the English fleet beginning to get underway, and he signaled his ships to raise anchor and withdraw as quickly as possible to the protection of shore batteries.

Howard, eager to force a battle, signaled to his fleet to launch an immediate attack on the two largest of the French ships. *Mary Rose*, with banners flying, led the way in the morning breeze toward *Grande Luise*. Men-at-arms aboard the English flagship

To the sound of cheers, the newly arrived one-hundred-ton *Germyne* anchored near *Mary Rose*, and her captain, Edward Echingham, was rowed over to the flagship. He was later quoted as saying, "I believe there was never a knight more welcome than I was to my lord admiral." The captain's cargo relieved the immediate crisis by providing ten days of food and drink.

The situation at Brest remained a standoff until the Mediterranean fleet's commander, Pregent de Bisdoux, attempted to break through Howard's line to enter the harbor. Although unsuccessful, the French attack cost Howard two of his ships, and Bisdoux managed to put a number of his men and artillery ashore. Howard's response was to land several hundred more men to counter this threat to his shore detachments and to renew the attempt on Brest. However, a swift reaction from the French garrison in the port effectively pinned down the lord admiral's new force. The galley fleet, meanwhile, continued to menace his rear.

Howard appeared to have few options by this time. In a fit of desperation, he decided to put twelve hundred of his men-at-arms into six shallow-draft oared boats, which had been carried aboard a number of his larger ships, and launch an attack on the harbor. He placed himself in the lead craft and boldly approached the French ships anchored under the protection of their shore batteries. Ignoring the odds, Howard refused to attempt to withdraw without having something to show Henry, and he urged the oarsmen on.

The French watched in disbelief as the small flotilla steadily approached their anchored ships. The moment the English were within range, French cannons and lighter guns on ship and shore roared a cruel greeting. Within minutes, the harbor was momentarily shrouded in smoke. The first French salvo blew one of Howard's boats out of the water, killing or wounding every man on board. All the other boats in the impromptu flotilla suffered some casualties. But despite the air being filled with, according to Echingham, "quarreles and gunstones that came as thick as hailstones," Howard continued with reckless courage toward the largest of the French ships before him, Clermont's flagship, *Grande Luise*. Managing to close the distance, he brought his small craft alongside his target.

Howard's crew, remembering the fate of *Regent*, threw a light anchor onto the enemy ship and lightly secured the line so that it could be easily cut free, if necessary. Simultaneously, Howard climbed up onto the enemy deck, followed by a Spanish cavalier who had volunteered to join him. Once aboard, Howard turned and called for his boarding party to follow him and the cavalier, though what he hoped to accomplish is difficult to imagine.

As it was, only sixteen Englishmen were able to board behind the lord admiral before the line holding their boat to the French ship parted or was cut. Howard watched in disbelief as his boat drifted away, leaving him isolated with a handful of men on the enemy deck. Turning

around, he could see French men-at-arms moving to encircle his small group.

Backing to the rail, Howard shouted to the men in his boat: "Come aboard again! Come aboard again!" But by then, the French pikemen had surrounded his small band and were spearing them cruelly. By some accounts, Howard took his golden whistle and chain from around his neck, the pipe being the insignia of his rank, and threw them into the water as a heroic gesture. Within minutes, everyone in the boarding party was either killed outright or thrown overboard to drown. The Englishmen in the other small boats watched in horror and immediately broke off their attack. Still under enemy fire, they rowed back to the safety of the larger ships and reboarded as quickly as possible. Later, when the French recovered Howard's torn body, they reported that his admiral's whistle was still around his neck, which of course casts doubt on the lord admiral's having made that final flourish.

Shocked by the sudden loss of their admiral, the English captains held a hurried conference aboard *Mary Rose*. Supplies were more critical than ever, and after a brief discussion, the consensus was they should retrieve the shore detachments and seek to abandon their blockade within a blockade. The Englishmen ashore and their cannons were recovered, and under cover of night, the English fleet managed to slip by the French galleys and head for Plymouth. On board the returning supply ship, *Germyne*, Captain Echingham penned a letter to Wolsey to explain what had happened.

It took time for Echingham's letter to reach Henry, and he was predictably furious on learning of the fleet's unauthorized flight from Brest. Although the would-be warrior king could discount the loss of Howard, he was embarrassed beyond belief at another incident of his forces withdrawing on their own authority, this also having been the outcome of the Aquitaine campaign. It would not be a happy homecoming for the fleet.

In London, there appeared to be no debate over Henry's decision to select the once passed-over Lord Thomas Howard II to replace his late brother as admiral. This time the choice was not difficult. The king needed to placate his nobility and gain someone of merit who could be counted on to bring personal vengeance to the task of leading the fleet. The new admiral also had to be willing to punish any of the English captains who may

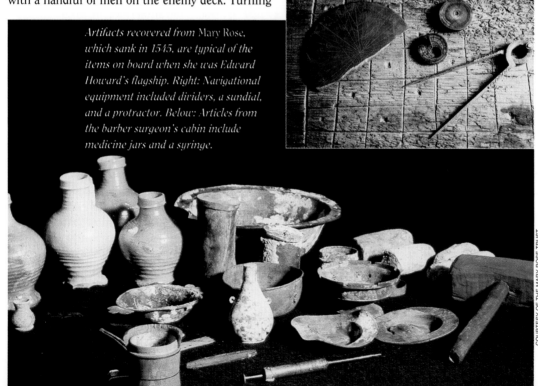

Artifacts recovered from Mary Rose, *which sank in 1545, are typical of the items on board when she was Edward Howard's flagship. Right: Navigational equipment included dividers, a sundial, and a protractor. Below: Articles from the barber surgeon's cabin include medicine jars and a syringe.*

have been derelict in their duty. Henry's commission was sent to Thomas Howard, inviting him to assume his late brother's office and command. These assignments would pay him two hundred pounds per annum (eighty thousand dollars—a third of the rate paid to his brother) and entitle him to claim all captured pirate booty. In an ironic turn as all this was being concluded, the French northern fleet came out of Brest Harbor and ventured across the Channel to invade the Sussex coast. The French were repulsed on the coastline, and their commander lost an eye to an arrow. Little was ever to be known or said about this raid.

Excited by the unexpected turnaround in his prospects (despite the pay differential), Thomas Howard left his new second wife at home and rode immediately to where the disgraced fleet lay at anchor in Plymouth Harbor. Arriving less than two weeks after his brother's death, the new lord admiral was rowed out to *Mary Rose*, riding quietly at anchor. Grim-faced, Howard climbed

After his brother's foolhardy death during the blockade of Brest, Thomas Howard (left) reported to the king's principal adviser, Bishop Thomas Wolsey (right), that the recent defeat was due to his brother's poor leadership. Wolsey, in turn, convinced King Henry not to release the report and instead to promote Edward Howard as a naval hero (Left: National Maritime Museum, Greenwich; Right: Mary Evans Picture Library).

aboard and ordered the returned captains to assemble there. The lord admiral proceeded to interrogate the officers closely, demanding to know why they had returned without permission. The captains tried to explain how limited supplies had forced their hand, pointing out that the next supply convoy had been held up in England by unfavorable winds. Those winds could, however, bring them home before supplies were exhausted.

The explanation was reasonable, but Howard refused to accept it. He sensed a lack of discipline, and the point about supplies was one he suspected Henry would never condone. As inexperienced as Henry was in military command, in his mind officers were expected to overcome difficulties—not hide behind them. Then, changing the subject, Howard put the toughest question of all to the fleet captains: Had they left their admiral, his brother, to be butchered?

The captains tried to answer all at once. Frowning deeply, Howard silenced them all in favor of a designated spokesman (probably Echingham), who then protested that every one of Edward's small vessels had taken losses in what amounted to a foolhardy attack. The spokesman also pointed out that the combined French fleets had outnumbered the English fleet. This fact left them at serious risk of being bottled up and destroyed if they did not withdraw without delay.

Later, Thomas Howard summarized his conclusions in a report to Wolsey. Expressing himself bluntly, he laid blame for the disaster on his late brother's faulty and inexperienced leadership, adding, "I have found here the worst-ordered army, filled with fear [of the French galleys]." He ended with the comment that he could not find it within himself to honor his brother's bravery or ill-advised daring. His willingness to be so critical would both please and annoy Henry.

Whatever had been Howard's intent, Wolsey quickly realized the report on Edward's command and death should never be released. Instead, he recommended to Henry that it be concealed

from the council. Wolsey reasoned that Edward Howard's death in battle gave a badly needed display of courage to rally the British. He encouraged Henry to talk about the war in terms of a tournament—one in which Englishmen could become heroes, like Edward Howard.

In the coming weeks, Wolsey spread the word that Lord Edward Howard had died bravely fighting for the honor of England. When the hero's will became public knowledge, it was discovered that he had left Henry one of his two ships, along with one of his two bastard sons—whichever the king might choose. Charles Brandon received the second of Edward's ships, the admiral's ceremonial chain of office made from three hundred gold coins, and whichever bastard son the king did not select. Again, Edward had completely ignored his family.

Sometime afterward, the French admiral returned Edward Howard's body to the English but kept his heart, to the shock of Henry VIII's council. This act provoked so much outrage that Wolsey was easily able to muster additional support for the war. The coming invasion of France through Calais, England's last vestige of its holdings in France, would be an expensive campaign.

England mourned its first naval hero, while Wolsey personally counted it fortunate that sixty-nine-year-old Thomas Howard I's influence upon the king was diminished by the loss of his second son and two sons-in-law, Knevet and Carew, all three of whom, of course, were great favorites of Henry. While the lord treasurer's influence with the king was surely lessened, Howard possibly did not mourn the loss of son Edward as much as Wolsey might have imagined. More likely, he saw Edward's death as God's punishment for his errant lifestyle and lack of respect for his father.

ROBERT L. SWAIN writes from New York City. This article is adapted from his forthcoming book on the life of Thomas Howard II, which is tentatively titled *A Tudor Survivor*.

Assigned to investigate Colonel John M. Chivington's Sand Creek attack (above), Ned Wynkoop reported that "the most fearful atrocities were committed that ever was heard of" (Colorado Historical Society).

Edward W. Wynkoop left Philadelphia in 1856 to seek his fortune in the West. Two years later the young man had made his way to "Bleeding Kansas," where the territory's governor, James W. Denver, appointed him sheriff for Arapahoe County, at the foot of the Rocky Mountains in what would become Colorado. At the center of a gold rush, the area boomed, and the infant town of Denver thrived. "Ned," as Wynkoop preferred to be called, had to live by his wits, and this involved running with a rough-and-tumble crowd.

Then two events transpired that would make it possible for him to change his lifestyle: the outbreak of the American Civil War and marriage. Wynkoop became an officer in the First Colorado Volunteer Infantry Regiment in July 1861, later fighting at the Battle of Glorieta Pass in New Mexico Territory. In August 1861 he married Louise Brown Wakely. His marriage, combined with the responsibility of command, matured

him. Still, he was unprepared for what was about to happen.

By 1864, the Confederates were replaced by a new foe: the Cheyennes, who called themselves the *Tsistsistas* (usually translated to mean "the People"), and their allies, who were terrorizing the southern Plains. Nearly all commerce ceased within the affected territories. Whites lived in fear. Wynkoop, by then a major, was ordered to command Fort Lyon, in southeastern Colorado Territory. Like most who migrated westward, he harbored the typical prejudices of the frontier—mainly, that Indians were less than human. Shortly after arriving at his new post on May 9, 1864, he received instructions from the commander of the District of Colorado, Colonel John Chivington. "The Cheyennes will have to be soundly whipped before they will be quiet," wrote Chivington. "If any of them are caught in your vicinity, kill them, as that is the only way."

Indian attacks continued, prompting Governor John Evans in Denver to write

Secretary of War Edwin Stanton, "One settlement devastated 25 miles east of here; murdered and scalped bodies brought in to-day." The governor went on to ask Stanton if he should "call a regiment of 100-days' men or muster into U.S. service the militia?" On August 13, the *Rocky Mountain News* printed Evans' proclamation that announced the enlistment of volunteers for one hundred days' service in the Third Colorado Volunteer Cavalry.

Although by fall Wynkoop had not yet engaged the enemy, he kept headquarters informed about their activities. In reporting one attempt to track down a band of Indian raiders, Wynkoop made clear his intentions: "At all events, it is my intention to kill all Indians I may come across until I receive orders to the contrary from headquarters." On September 4, some of his soldiers brought three captured Cheyennes to Fort Lyon. Wynkoop was outraged, for the soldiers had not obeyed his orders to kill any Indians they encountered.

Then one of the captives, One Eye, handed Wynkoop a letter, written by half-blood George Bent, requesting a council at which Cheyenne and Arapaho leaders could talk peace. "I thought I would be

tinct warrior society within the Cheyenne tribe. They welcomed any warrior willing to fight white aggression.

Wynkoop, caught unprepared, hurriedly formed his own battle line and continued to advance. Before any fighting broke out, however, Cheyenne leader Black Kettle sent word that Cheyenne and Arapaho leaders would meet the white chief in council the next day.

to laugh at us, nor does he regard us as children, but, on the contrary, unlike the balance of his race, he comes with confidence in the pledges given by the red man. He has been told by one of our bravest warriors that he should come and go unharmed...." The Indian leader, who was about sixty-one years old, told Major Wynkoop to withdraw with his troopers and not halt his command

Between the Army

Ned Wynkoop arrived in the West with commonly held prejudices against Indians, but as an army officer and Indian agent he championed peace during the bloody southern Plains wars.

and the Cheyennes

by Louis Kraft

killed," One Eye said, "but I knew that paper would be found upon my dead body, that you would see it, and it might give peace to my people once more." One Eye assured Wynkoop that he would not be harmed, and that the Indians would release white captives to him. One Eye's words and courage in pursuing peace deeply moved Wynkoop and marked the beginning of a transformation of his attitude toward the Indians. He later wrote of the incident: "I was bewildered with an exhibition of such patriotism....These were the representatives of a race that I had heretofore looked upon without exception as being cruel[,] treacherous, and blood-thirsty...."

Wynkoop, ignoring the advice of his officers, rode out with interpreter John Smith and 127 soldiers on September 6 to meet with the natives at the Smoky Hill River in Kansas. Four days later he found the Indians, drawn up in a formidable battle line of six hundred to eight hundred warriors. Present among them were Dog Soldiers, members of a dis-

The gathering did not go as planned. The Indian leaders glared at Wynkoop, their hatred and contempt for this white soldier obvious. (In his memoirs, Wynkoop went so far as to describe them as "snarling wolves.") The major told them that he "was not authorized to conclude peace terms with them." Wynkoop then said that if they gave him the white prisoners in their possession, he would take their chiefs to Denver to meet Governor Evans. He closed by guaranteeing their safe return.

A large chief leaped to his feet and demanded to know why the white man thought the Cheyennes were fools to give up something without anything in return. An eruption of anger ensued among the Indians, and violence seemed imminent. Before blows could be struck, however, One Eye admonished the Indians not to harm the white man.

Then Black Kettle spoke up for the first time, demanding silence. The chief stood and, according to an Indian account, said: "This white man is not here

until sundown, then to await the Cheyennes' decision.

As promised, the white captives were delivered: sixteen-year-old Laura Roper and three younger children, Isabella Eubanks, Ambrose Asher, and Daniel Marble. Seven Cheyenne and Arapaho chiefs, including Black Kettle, agreed to go to Denver to talk peace.

The meeting took place at Camp Weld, on the outskirts of the city, on September 28. Black Kettle spoke eloquently of his desire for peace. Next, Governor Evans brought up the Cheyennes' alliance with the Sioux—which Black Kettle denied—and the depredations committed by the Indians. He then said that the Indians' time of war was summer and that his time of war was winter. When Evans stated that the Indians would have to make peace with the military, Black Kettle said he could not talk for all his warriors, whereupon Wynkoop quickly reminded him that the Dog Soldiers had said they would support his decision.

ATTENTION!
INDIAN
FIGHTERS

Having been authorized by the Governor to raise a Company of 100 day

U. S. VOL CAVALRY!

For immediate service against hostile Indians. I call upon all who wish to engage in such service to call at my office and enroll their names immediately.

Pay and Rations the same as other U. S. Volunteer Cavalry.

Parties furnishing their own horses will receive 40c per day, and rations for the same, while in the service.

The Company will also be entitled to all horses and other plunder taken from the Indians.

Office first door East of Recorder's Office.

HAL SAYR.

Central City, Aug. 13, '64.

Indian attacks against white settlements compelled Colorado Territory Governor John Evans to request the War Department's permission to raise a regiment for one hundred days' service. Soon broadsides appealing for volunteers to join the new unit appeared around Denver.

Finally, the governor implored them, saying, "Whatever peace you make must be with the soldiers, and not with me." Closing the council, Chivington said, "You are nearer Major Wynkoop than any one else, and you can go to him when you get ready to do that." Wynkoop and the chiefs were elated, as peace was seemingly at hand. They returned to Fort Lyon, and the leaders left to move their villages near the post.

Evans, however, saw the meeting differently and told Cheyenne agent Samuel G. Colley, "I have declined to make any treaty with them, lest it might embarrass the military operations against the hostile Indians of the plains." According to Wynkoop, Evans had told him just prior to the meeting that if peace was achieved before the Third Colorado took the field, Washington would conclude that "there had never been any necessity for the government to go to the expense of raising that regiment."

A month later, Wynkoop was suddenly relieved of duty at Fort Lyon and ordered to report to District of the Upper Arkansas headquarters at Fort Riley, Kansas. There he learned that he had violated the dictum: "Commanders of Posts and their subordinates will not inaugurate or send out military expeditions without orders from these Head Quarters." Wynkoop later testified that Maj. Gen. Samuel R. Curtis told him that he had been censured "for committing an unmilitary act by leaving my district without orders and proceeding to Denver City with the Indian chiefs and white captives to the governor of Colorado instead of coming to myself...."

On November 28, two days after Wynkoop had left Fort Lyon, Chivington and the Third Colorado, the one hundred days' regiment, arrived there. The colonel demanded that a detachment of the First Colorado Cavalry join them in an attack upon the Cheyenne-Arapaho village, which was then more than thirty miles away on Sand Creek. The November 29 dawn attack butchered Indians who thought they were at peace with the whites. Chivington proclaimed a major victory, and his initial report claimed five hundred Indians died. Cheered as saviors, the troopers paraded through Denver with the genitals of the dead dangling from their shirts and hats.

Smoking a cigar, Wynkoop squats directly in front of Cheyenne Chief Black Kettle in a photograph taken on September 28, 1864, during peace talks with Governor Evans. Captain Silas Soule, kneeling, was later present at Sand Creek, but Chivington rebuked him for "saying that he thanked God that he had killed no Indians, and like expressions."

Indians. He no longer considered them less than human.

Chivington's attack did not end the war; instead, it intensified it. The southern Plains dripped with blood during 1865, as the Cheyennes and their allies struck back. In October, the U.S. government appointed a peace commission to meet with the warring tribes. To his surprise and shock, Wynkoop was ordered to command its military escort. He figured that the Cheyennes held him responsible for the disaster at Sand Creek, but Wynkoop could not have been more mistaken. Instead of blaming him, they were glad to see him. A day after his arrival on the Little Arkansas River, Black Kettle invited him to his lodge. He told the major that "not for one moment had any of them doubts of [Wynkoop's] good faith." Before the conference ended and the Treaty of the Little Arkansas was signed, the Cheyennes named Wynkoop "the Tall Chief" because of his height, six feet three inches. He was also known as the "Man Who Will Not Tell a Lie."

The treaty specified a new reservation south of the Arkansas River while granting the Cheyennes the right to continue to hunt north of the river, and it also marked the beginning of the end of Wynkoop's military service. The government had come to realize just how valuable he was in dealing with Indians and placed him on detached service. By the end of the year, he was made special agent to the Cheyennes—his sole duty to bring native militants to the council fire.

This was not an easy task. The nomadic bands were spread over a massive area. Bad weather did not help matters. Finally, on February 28, 1866, Wynkoop met approximately four thousand Indians on Bluff Creek in southern Kansas. Black Kettle, whom Wynkoop now considered a friend, was present, as was the Cheyenne mystic and chief Stone Forehead and a number of Dog Soldier leaders. Neither Stone Forehead nor the Dog Soldiers

Wynkoop, livid when he heard the news, was transferred back to Fort Lyon, brevetted a lieutenant colonel, and tasked with investigating the so-called massacre. The horrors committed at Sand Creek left a lasting impression on him. In his report Wynkoop called the affair an "unprecedented atrocity" in which "women and children were killed and scalped, children shot at their mothers' breasts, and all the bodies mutilated in the most horrible manner." He concluded that Chivington, "this inhuman monster," was clearly to blame for the massacre. All told, about two hundred Indians were killed, some two-thirds of whom were women and children. The investigation failed to prosecute Chivington, who retired from the army. On a personal level, the tragedy completed the change in Wynkoop's perception of

With a greatcoat rakishly thrown over a shoulder, Wynkoop stood for his portrait shortly after joining the First Colorado Infantry Regiment in 1861.

was pleased about the Kansas Pacific Railroad cutting through their hunting grounds along the Smoky Hill River—and they were even more unhappy about giving up their land and living south of the Arkansas. Nevertheless, Wynkoop persuaded them to agree to the Little Arkansas Treaty, and they touched the paper. He was also able to secure the release of sixteen-year-old Mary Fletcher, who had been captured the previous August.

While this council took place, a war party appeared on Smoky Hill, demonstrating one of the difficulties in negotiating peace: Chiefs did not speak for everyone in their tribe. Wynkoop immediately sent out runners, inviting the newly arrived warriors to meet with him. They agreed, and that council took place at Wood Creek on April 4.

When Porcupine Bear stood during the meeting, an unnerved Wynkoop grabbed his revolver and started to pull it from his holster. Luckily, he realized in time that Porcupine Bear only stood to speak—and released his grip on his weapon before anyone noticed his aggressive action. Wynkoop's talent for making his listeners believe him worked again, and he obtained additional signatures. Less than a week later, Wynkoop wrote to the *Rocky Mountain News*: "I have now seen every single hostile Indian of the Arapaho and Cheyenne nations, and have concluded what they themselves are pleased to term, a 'strong peace.'"

No matter what he accomplished, however, it was never enough. Perhaps the natives' promises to keep the peace and walk the white man's road were sincere, but certain factions within the tribes would not keep those pledges. Hostilities soon resumed along the Smoky Hill, with Dog Soldiers harassing whites who trespassed on what they considered to be their land. Although Wynkoop was accused by some Indians of misleading them in order to secure their treaty signatures, more likely the natives realized they could not give up their beloved land even though they wanted peace. Nevertheless, despite isolated incidents and accusations, peace reigned throughout most of 1866.

Wynkoop, however, saw that he walked a precarious line between the races and that no matter what agreements he persuaded both sides to sign, they would ei-ther be blocked by officials in Washington or denied by Indians who refused to give up what they regarded as theirs by birthright. He soon realized that he could not continue in his current position. On July 11, Wynkoop resigned his military commission and traveled east to meet with President Andrew Johnson, who appointed him agent of the Upper Arkansas Agency, headquartered at Fort Larned, Kansas. His wards included the Southern Cheyennes, the Arapahos, and the Plains Apaches.

Although 1866 ended with a noticeable reduction in violence between whites and Indians, race relations remained strained as white encroachment continued into 1867. For that reason, as well as to secure the Plains for the coming of railroads, the U.S. government decided that a show of force was necessary to persuade the tribes on the central and southern Plains that they must do as instructed by white authorities. Major General Winfield S. Hancock, a Civil War hero and commander of the Department of the Missouri, organized an expedition, which included the Seventh U.S. Cavalry, commanded by Lt. Col. George A. Custer, to meet with leaders from the various tribes. On March 13, 1867, Hancock asked Wynkoop to set up a meeting with his wards at Fort Larned. The agent made the arrangements, but a snowstorm prevented the Cheyenne and Dog Soldier chiefs from meeting Hancock on April 10.

Chivington resigned from the army in January 1865 and escaped punishment for his central role in the Sand Creek massacre (Colorado Historical Society).

Dog Soldier Chiefs Tall Bull, White Horse, and Bull Bear, Cheyenne Chief Little Robe, Oglala Sioux Chief Pawnee Killer, and ten or so other Indian leaders eventually appeared at Larned on the night of April 12. Even though peace councils always took place during daylight hours, Hancock insisted that the worn-out leaders meet with him that same night. After a pipe was lighted and shared, Hancock told the leaders, "We [a]re not [here] to make war, but [a]re ready…to fight any Indians who [wish] for war." He then said that he intended to visit their village. Hancock had fifteen hundred men under his command—his threat was obvious.

A little after midnight, Wynkoop, upon Tall Bull's request, asked Hancock not to move toward the village, but his words fell on deaf ears. Hancock set out for the Indian encampment the next morning. Cheyennes joined Wynkoop during the march, warning him that their women and children, fearing another massacre, would panic when the troops reached their village. Wynkoop again passed on the message, but Hancock would not be denied. Even a prairie fire failed to halt his advance. About noon on April 13, Hancock's army climbed a small hill to find a massive line of some three hundred Cheyenne and Sioux warriors awaiting him in the valley below. The soldiers deployed for battle.

"The whole command presented such an appearance as I have seen just prior to the opening of an engagement," Wynkoop later wrote. Acting quickly, he rode to Hancock and told him the Cheyennes' fears would be eased if they knew he was present. For once Hancock agreed. Wynkoop took Edmund Guerrier, a half-blood Cheyenne interpreter, and rode into the valley.

Most of the Cheyennes dashed forward to meet him and expressed "their delight at seeing me there," Wynkoop reported, "saying that now they knew everything was all right, and they would not be harmed." Nevertheless, everyone in the camp was nervous and angry. Even though many of the Indians trusted his word, he knew others blamed him for the Sand Creek attack.

When Wynkoop saw the famed Cheyenne warrior Roman Nose riding back and forth in front of the native line,

More than five thousand Indians and six hundred whites, including scores of reporters and artists, attended the peace treaty talks at Medicine Lodge Creek. By then an Indian agent, Wynkoop escorted the government's peace commissioners to the gathering (Library of Congress).

screaming at the Indians to fight, he galloped to him and asked him to keep his warriors from attacking. He then led Roman Nose and eleven other Indian leaders toward the white line to meet Hancock and his officers.

The army commander told the Indians that if they had come to fight, he was ready to commence. After complaining about the difficulty of speaking and understanding each other on the windswept hillside, Hancock said he would talk after moving closer to the village.

The meeting over, the natives raced to their village, and Hancock resumed his march. Wynkoop approached the general and asked him to reconsider closing on the village, adding, "I [fear] the result [will] be the flight of the women and children...." But Hancock continued on until he reached the encampment—132 Cheyenne and 140 Sioux lodges—on the Pawnee Fork. Wynkoop had been right: The women frantically packed their ponies, grabbed their children, and fled.

That night, Hancock ordered Custer to capture the village, which he did. The warriors, however, had also departed. Left behind was only one girl, variously reported as being white, half blood, or Cheyenne, who had been raped.

Wynkoop hounded Hancock all night. When the general stated his intention to burn the village, Wynkoop said that his wards were innocent of any wrongdoing and did not deserve such punishment. He added, "I am fully convinced that the

result would be an Indian outbreak of the most serious nature." Frustrated, Wynkoop returned to his tent and wrote a protest letter to Hancock. He also wrote to Commissioner of Indian Affairs Nathaniel G. Taylor, predicting another war. Hancock, again ignoring Wynkoop's advice, burned the village on April 19.

The agent lashed out at the wanton destruction in a letter to Thomas Murphy, superintendent of Indian Affairs: "General Hancock has declared war upon the Cheyennes, and ordered all to be shot who make their appearance north of the Arkansas or south of the Platte Rivers. The question is, what have these Indians done to cause such action?"

As Wynkoop had predicted, war returned to the area. Although the agent remained in the field to "exert myself to further the public interests as long as I hold the position I now occupy," it quickly became too dangerous for him to travel among his charges. Beginning in June, he stayed at Larned. Among the Indians' main grievances was the construction of the Kansas Pacific Railroad, which was snaking its way along the Smoky Hill toward Colorado Territory. Wynkoop remained convinced that the war would once again result in the slaughter of innocent people. As fall approached, another peace council was arranged—at Medicine Lodge Creek in Kansas.

Wynkoop and Murphy arrived at the council grounds on September 14. Already fourteen hundred Indians had ar-

rived—Kiowas, Comanches, Arapahos, and Plains Apaches. Only those Cheyennes who followed Black Kettle's lead were present.

When Wynkoop and Murphy learned that Stone Forehead had called for a ritual gathering of other Cheyennes thirty miles to the south on the Cimarron River to renew their Sacred Arrows, they invited him to attend the council as well. The mystic refused—the sacred ceremony had to be completed before the Cheyennes could attend the council.

Meanwhile, other Indians arrived daily at Medicine Lodge Creek. One night while Wynkoop ate with Black Kettle, Murphy, and George Bent, Roman Nose and ten warriors raided the camp, intending to kill the Indian agent. Luckily for Wynkoop, Arapahos learned of Roman Nose's intentions and delayed him just long enough for Wynkoop to leap on a horse and escape to Fort Larned and safety.

Shortly after Wynkoop's hasty return to Larned, the government's peace commissioners arrived there. They were frightened, as antagonistic Cheyennes had burned the prairie in an attempt to forestall their journey. Wynkoop's charm surfaced—along with his private supply of alcohol—and he managed to lift their spirits. On October 12, Wynkoop and the commissioners, including Senator John B. Henderson of Missouri and retired General William S. Harney, left for Medicine Lodge, arriving two days later. By the time they reached the encampment,

On November 27, 1868, the army attacked Black Kettle's Washita River village, killing the chief and some one hundred others. Two days later, frustrated at the government's broken promises and unable to alter the army's policy of extermination, Wynkoop resigned as Indian agent.

the whites numbered six hundred, while the native population had grown to five thousand. Black Kettle warned of an attack, and almost everyone suffered through a sleepless night.

On the night of October 16, the commissioners called Wynkoop before them to give his reasons for the recent war. After pointing out that Hancock's April burning of the Pawnee Fork village had ignited the summer war, the agent said that unscrupulous government officials cheated his wards. Often, their annuities consisted of half-full barrels of sugar, rotted blankets, and clothing that was foreign to Indians, such as women's bonnets. "The Indians told me," Wynkoop said, "they would not have taken those [inferior] goods from anybody else but myself." He concluded by stating that fully two-thirds of the goods promised were never delivered.

The council finally began on the nineteenth. After native leaders and Murphy spoke, Senator Henderson told the Indians that the buffalo would soon be gone and that they should live like white men and plow Mother Earth. Not one Indian present wanted to adopt that way of life. The Comanches and Kiowas never-

theless signed treaties on October 21 in which they agreed to live on a reservation in what is modern southwestern Kansas and were allowed to hunt along the Big Bend of the Arkansas River and the Texas Panhandle. The Plains Apaches asked to live with them on their new reservation. Days passed. Still, there was no sign of the missing Cheyennes. Then, on October 27, a dust cloud billowed ominously to the south of the encampment. Soldiers from the Seventh Cavalry prepared for battle as colorfully painted and dressed warriors appeared among the trees, charged across the water, and formed a battle line. But there would be no fight that day. The missing Cheyennes had completed their ceremony and arrived, ready to listen to what the whites had to say.

The council continued the next day. Only Dog Soldier leader Buffalo Chief spoke, making it clear that his people would never give up the land between the Arkansas and South Platte Rivers. Henderson took the Cheyenne leaders aside and assured them they could hunt buffalo north of the Arkansas for as long as there were buffalo. Of course, as the *New York Times* reported, the treaty

stated the opposite—"[the] voluntary abandonment of the country between the Arkansas and Platte rivers."

The Arapahos and Cheyennes made their marks on the treaty. Before the ink could dry, however, Seventh Cavalry Captain Albert Barnitz wrote in his journal, "[The Indians] have no idea... that they have...given up the...country north of the Arkansas."

By February 1868, Wynkoop's wards were congregated sixty miles south of the Arkansas. Although peaceful, they did have a complaint: The arms and ammunition promised them at the Medicine Lodge conference had not been delivered. Wynkoop set out for their villages on February 4, finding the Indians "in a very destitute condition—almost starving," and issued annuities. Addressing rumors that had recently surfaced in the East that his wards were again hostile, he emphatically reported, "I beg to inform the department, [these reports] are absolutely false."

Of course, the government would not keep its part of the Treaty of Medicine Lodge. By June, a full nine months after the treaty had been signed, Congress had still not ratified it—that would not happen until July 25. By then, it was too late. Wynkoop's wards were in serious straits, many close to starvation. Add to that their demoralization as a result of the continued encroachment upon their lands by white settlers, and it is little wonder that an explosion was imminent.

It would get worse. The government ordered Wynkoop not to deliver any arms or ammunition during the next distribution of goods. His next visit to the Cheyenne camps did not go well when the Indians realized he did not bring weapons. Eventually, the flow of supplies also stopped, making the arms an even greater necessity if the Indians were to secure their own food.

The tense situation erupted after a Cheyenne war party, which had set out to raid the Pawnees, attacked whites along the Solomon and Saline Rivers in Kansas. Wynkoop knew that this was just what the government wanted—an excuse to attack his wards. Disregarding his own safety, he immediately set out for the Cheyenne villages. Finding Stone Forehead and Little Rock, he got right to the point— the guilty parties must be handed over to the government for punishment. Surprisingly, they agreed.

Wynkoop's efforts to maintain peace, however, again failed. Before the chiefs had a chance to deliver the raiders, a punitive army expedition headed by Brig. Gen. Alfred Sully was in the field. War once again swept across the Plains. At a loss as to what to do, Wynkoop fled east to Philadelphia. All his efforts for peace had failed.

That fall Wynkoop was ordered back to the frontier and tasked with gathering his Indian wards at Fort Cobb in Indian Territory and distributing food to them. Wynkoop had set out to do so when suddenly his orders were changed. He was instructed "…to distribute no annuities to any…Indians unless they give up, without ransom, all white captives now held by them" and agree to forever live on a reservation. Moreover, five armed columns were already moving toward the Washita River, where it was suspected that the Cheyennes were wintering. More disturbing to Wynkoop, the Nineteenth Kansas Volunteer Cavalry, which

had been organized in October for the sole purpose of killing Indians, had also entered the field. Memories of Sand Creek and Pawnee Fork haunted Wynkoop, and his conscience would not allow him to take part in what he suspected the future held. On November 29, 1868, while still en route to Cobb, he wrote that the Cheyennes "will readily respond to my call, but I most certainly refuse to again be the instrument of the murder of innocent women and chil-

Wynkoop (left), depicted with his interpreter John Smith at the Pawnee Fork in April 1867, refused to temper his anger over the government's inhumanity toward the Indians and the Washita attack, which he wrote the commissioner of Indian Affairs was "wrong and disgraceful" (Harper's Weekly).

dren….All left me under the circumstances, with the present state of feelings I have in this matter, is now to respectfully tender my resignation."

Unknown to him, Wynkoop's prediction had already become reality. On November 27, the Seventh Cavalry attacked Black Kettle's village on the Washita River in Indian Territory. Black Kettle and more than one hundred other Indians were killed that day. When Wynkoop heard the news, he was both saddened and outraged. Black Kettle had been a friend as well as a man of great integrity.

On December 14, the U.S. Senate opened an investigation into the attack

on the Washita. By January 5, 1869, the senators had only collected a handful of documents, most of which were submitted by Murphy and Wynkoop. The former agent's papers clearly showed that time and again his wards had been forced into a hostile attitude. His efforts to bring forth the truth, however, collided head-on with a seemingly impregnable wall. Those who opposed Wynkoop's views dismissed him as part of the so-called "Indian Ring," a group of miscreants who had grown rich using the government to milk the Indians for every penny. That gambit was unfair but effective, as it swept away Wynkoop's words almost before he uttered them.

In January 1869 Wynkoop returned to Philadelphia. Although he had resigned his commission, he refused to walk away from what he considered a travesty. With a letter from one of his interpreters, J.S. Morrison, in hand, on January 26, 1869, he wrote Indian Affairs Commissioner Taylor regarding the attack at Washita. His closing was scathing: "Mr. Morrison states that there are 40 women and children killed. That fact needs no comment; it speaks for itself. I do not know whether the government desires to look at this office in a humane light or not, and if it only desires to know whether it was right or wrong to attack the village referred to, I must emphatically pronounce it wrong and disgraceful."

Wynkoop would later drift back to the West, serving as captain of the Black Hills Rangers and working as a timber agent, but his refusal to remain quiescent—in particular his barrage of statements regarding what he considered the murder of innocent people—had ended his chance to remain an influential voice of reason and fairness in dealing with the Indians. His bid to become commissioner of Indian Affairs fell on deaf ears. And the Cheyennes lost perhaps the best white friend they ever had.

LOUIS KRAFT is the author of *Custer and the Cheyenne: George Armstrong Custer's Winter Campaign on the Southern Plains* (Upton & Sons, 1995).

THEY REMAINED
Filipino Guerrillas in World War II

Enduring brutal Japanese reprisals, resistance fighters kept the hope for democracy alive in the Philippines and paved the way for Douglas MacArthur's triumphant return.

by John W. Whitman

The New Year began badly for Filipinos. January 1942 witnessed the fall of Manila to the Japanese. In April, Bataan fell. In May, Corregidor and the southern Philippines surrendered. The Japanese had, in just five months, wiped American military forces from the Philippine Islands. Their next step would be incorporation of the island's people and resources into their empire.

General Douglas MacArthur, commander of United States Army Forces in the Far East (USAFFE), had reluctantly departed the country, as had Commonwealth President Manuel Quezon. The Filipinos had good reasons to question their allegiance to the United States. Filipino officials remaining in Manila had instructions to cooperate with the Japanese so as to protect the public. It seemed to the country's residents that America was sending its combat forces to other theaters and deliberately avoiding the Philippines. Even so, from the moment the Japanese took Manila, Filipinos everywhere passively resisted the invaders. Whether or not that resistance would turn active depended a great deal on the Japanese.

The Japanese quickly ruined any chance they had to win over their new subjects. Even as propagandists promised independence and a new day for Asians, Japanese sentries slapped and kicked Filipinos who failed to bow properly. Property and food theft by Japanese soured the Filipinos' attitudes toward Japan's Greater East Asia Co-prosperity Sphere. Filipinos renamed it the Greater

East Asia Robbery Sphere. Japanese swords drew blood within days of arriving in Manila. The mere suspicion of being a looter or a member of the resistance meant death, and beheadings ended hundreds of lives in the first months of the occupation. No proof or judicial proceedings were needed.

The Japanese never tried to understand the Filipinos. Communiqués were blunt and threatening. Even when friendly, the Japanese were racist, condescending, and patronizing. They professed friendship and Asiatic love for their Filipino brothers and claimed that Japan's war was only against the Americans, but they followed up their words with brutality, injustice, and deadly force. The Japanese wanted to immediately undo American colonialism, but their abrupt attempt to supplant democratic ideas with totalitarian practices inflamed the populace.

Filipinos stopped waiting for American salvation after U.S. forces on Corregidor and in the southern islands surrendered, but few took to the hills in a rush of patriotic fever. More often it required first-hand experience with the Japanese to turn the Filipinos to armed resistance. Rationing, price controls, and the daily insecurity of life and property drove them to defend themselves. Beatings, verbal abuse, and face slappings began the moment Japanese soldiers entered a town. When the Japanese hired informers, they paid them well, with bonuses for especially important information. That system became so successful that in some areas cooperation with guerrillas was instantly reported to the Japanese. Also helpful in secret police work were longtime Japanese residents of the Philippines who knew the islands. Unjustified arrests and executions, corporal punishment, kidnappings, rape, and theft built a burning desire in Filipinos to avenge their wrongs.

Even before conventional resistance ended, guerrilla groups had begun to form. The islands offered rough, isolated terrain on which to organize, yet food was within reach. Early in 1942, weak Japanese garrisons could not prevent bands from operating with near impunity. Guerrilla bands coalesced around anyone bold enough to take charge.

An American cavalry captain who had been cut off during the retreat to Bataan formed one such band, then attacked two Japanese airfields, destroyed numerous aircraft, and killed airfield personnel. An American colonel in north Luzon obtained authority from MacArthur on Corregidor to raise a regiment. A Filipino captain collected remnants of a regiment and linked up with other men. An American miner gathered Filipino soldiers, U.S. radar operators cut off by enemy landings, and civilians. They ambushed Japanese troops, tossed dynamite into billets, and generally raised hell throughout the mountains. These Filipinos were not about to stand idly aside. "When the war is over," said a young Filipino lawyer, "my boys will ask me what I did to help free my country. I cannot tell them that I had no part in it." Many Filipinos who had not retreated to Bataan banded together and went into hiding.

After Bataan fell, and while the fortress of Corregidor held out, men who had refused to surrender hiked through Japanese lines and headed for the hills of north Luzon. Scores of Americans and Filipinos wandered north. Some men escaped from the deadly Bataan Death March. Filipino civilians sheltered, fed, and helped these men, always at great risk to themselves and their families.

The formal fall of the Philippines in May 1942 failed to end armed resistance. Even after Lt. Gen. Jonathan M. Wainwright finally enforced his surrender de-

Barefoot and shirtless, Filipino guerrillas march down a Mindinaoan road on May 11, 1945. Engaged mostly in gathering intelligence during the Japanese occupation, resistance fighters went on the offensive after U.S. troops returned to the Philippine Islands (National Archives).

Above: Crouching Japanese soldiers sprint past the camera as they assault a U.S. position on the main Philippine island of Luzon in early 1942. On Luzon, outnumbered U.S. and Filipino troops fell back to the Bataan Peninsula and the island of Corregidor. The Allied commander in the Philippines, Lt. Gen. Jonathan M. Wainwright, finally capitulated on May 6, 1942, and endured further humiliation when the Japanese forced him to broadcast surrender instructions from a Manila radio station (right). Although most units surrendered (below), thousands of Filipino and American troops slipped through Japanese lines to the mountains, where as guerrillas they continued to resist the invaders.

once the conventional military forces dissolved.

On the island of Panay, Colonel Albert F. Christie's Sixty-first Division had only a modicum of training, and discipline was deplorable. Arms, ammunition, medicine, vehicles, and signal equipment had failed to arrive in necessary quantities. But food supplies were adequate, and Japanese military operations had so far failed to pressure his men. Christie stocked mountain retreats with food, fuel, and even machine shops. Log and bamboo warehouses held six months' worth of supplies.

On May 10 Christie was shocked to receive orders to surrender his command. The division commander questioned why he should capitulate because "some other unit has gone to hell or some Corregidor shell-shocked terms" had been reached. While dragging out the surrender process, Christie gave Filipino operations officer Colonel Macario Peralta one hundred thousand pesos to start an underground movement. News spread of Peralta's refusal to surrender. Many Filipinos believed Christie had been captured rather than surrender. Thus, the surrender order was seen as void, and many natives and Americans refused to comply.

In fact, by the time Christie finally capitulated, about 90 percent of his men had slipped off into the mountains to continue the struggle as guerrillas or had gone home. With them went their weapons and the limited amount of ammunition available. A few battalions and companies remained nearly intact and re-formed under their former officers. When some Filipinos actually did surrender, the Japanese generally released the enlisted men and allowed them to return home. The early establishment of guerrilla command and control paralleled the continuation of civil government under vigorous civilian leaders. Ample space in the island's interior, plenty of time to organize, and a weak Japanese garrison got the resistance movement up and running in record time.

cision on American commanders in the southern islands, the Japanese still had problems. In December 1941, Brig. Gen. William F. Sharp, commander of the Visayan-Mindanao Force, had received orders from MacArthur to hold out as long as possible and then begin guerrilla warfare. Although the Japanese invaders had not yet arrived on the Visayan Islands, Brig. Gen. Bradford G. Chynoweth initiated a program there dubbed Operation *Baus Au*, Visayan for "Get it back."

On Panay and Cebu, Chynoweth began large-scale movements of food, materiel, and weapons into the islands' interiors. His troops cached equipment and food at inaccessible mountain hideouts at the end of narrow trails that hardly accommodated a single man on foot. Although such preparations initially demoralized the Filipinos—brave but inexperienced and untrained men who wanted to destroy the Japanese on the beaches—these stocks proved valuable

Surrender of USAFFE forces occurred without delay on the big island of Mindanao. Even so, large numbers of soldiers simply walked away rather than become prisoners of war. Later in 1942, the Japanese released Filipinos who had survived the horrible prisoner of war camps on Luzon. The sick and emaciated survivors staggered home. Many of them rested only long enough to regain their strength before they either became guerrillas or resumed their prewar jobs in towns and cities. There, they built and operated intelligence networks.

After the conquest, the Japanese pulled troops out and sent them to more active theaters south of the Philippines. By necessity, they left towns under the control of puppet constabulary troops and some prewar officials. Because USAFFE's conventional forces had not contested Japanese landings on the islands, Filipino soldiers reached the hills often with weapons, ammunition and supplies. According to former soldier Vicente Sydiongco:

Our military unit never faced the Japanese in a military confrontation except in two instances when we fired at unidentified planes before the surrender and disbandment of our company in May 1942. I became a member of the Leyte guerrilla forces sometime in October of that year….Our initial guerrilla unit was organized by a retired Philippine Scout. There were two such units operating in the area, made up of men with previous military experiences, ones who had arms and ammunition and commissions in the defunct Philippine army and U.S. Army, college students, high school kids and close relatives of those already guerrilla leaders.

Where the invaders lightly occupied or had not penetrated an area, local anti-Japanese constabularies and volunteers filled the vacuum. A few guerrilla groups used terror to organize their bases of support. Others recognized existing civilian leaders, organized civilian agencies, and established civilian governments. Groups sometimes banded together, with stronger ones absorbing

Filipino children stare out from what was once their home. Filipino civilians endured untold hardships during Japan's brutal occupation. Often unable to track down guerrillas, Japanese troops vented their frustration on civilians, whom they tortured and executed and whose homes they destroyed.

NATIONAL ARCHIVES

weaker units, either by peaceful agreement or by force. Although there was jealousy and strife, they hated the Japanese more than they hated each other.

But not always. Civilians feared some guerrilla bands more than they did the Japanese. The Hukbalahap ("Huks"), the People's Anti-Japanese Army, was one of the largest and most powerful guerrilla organizations in central Luzon. It owed allegiance to neither the United States nor the Philippine Commonwealth, refused to cooperate with other guerrilla bands, and had a strong Communist philosophy.

On Leyte, a fierce rivalry erupted between two guerrilla groups, one commanded by Lt. Col. Ruperto K. Kangleon and the other by Brig. Gen. Blas E. Miranda. A twenty-seven-year Philippine army veteran, Kangleon was so hostile to the Japanese that he killed many former Filipino prisoners of the invaders for fear that they were spies. Aggravating the rivalry was the fact that Miranda was a former Japanese prisoner. After tensions had built and Kangleon had threatened to "force…Miranda to join us," the colonel ordered an attack in which guerrillas killed guerrillas and the general's forces were routed, leaving Kangleon as guerrilla commander of the island.

During the years of occupation, the guerrillas and the Filipino people formed an interdependent relationship. Leaders of resistance groups and the civilian government ruled both towns and countryside wherever the Japanese were weak. Parts of Mindanao operated through 1942 and into 1943 as if the Japanese were not a factor. After guerrillas and vigilantes had suppressed banditry, Filipino civil servants returned to their prewar duties. Telephones and telegraphs sent messages over hundreds of miles. Farmers doubled their crops, so as to feed guerrillas. Small boats carried merchandise from one coastal bay to the next. Most guerrilla bands, like Sydiongco's, got their food from civilians, paying when they could but commandeering food when they had no money. On parts of Leyte, guerrilla units had more control over civilian activities and were in charge of allotting food supplies and even issuing emergency currency.

After the guerrillas had organized themselves—generally by mid-1942—they drove small Japanese garrisons out of interior towns. And once the resisters had become strong enough to suppress widespread banditry and to extend their control over more territory, more of the populace rallied to their side. Public ceremonies and the raising of American and Philippine Commonwealth flags marked the liberation of each town.

No central headquarters in the Philippines organized these bands. No unified command gave them guidance, supplied them, or equipped them. Everything was local. If the guerrilla resistance was to mean anything to the American cause, however, it had to feed information to MacArthur's headquarters in Australia. But how could the guerrillas and officials in Australia communicate?

In mid-1942 all MacArthur's radio operators could do was listen. The first message to reach the general came in June from Filipino Major Guillermo Z. Nakar, who was operating in central Luzon with a group of Americans and Filipinos who had refused to surrender. Unfortunately, this source of information was short-lived. Australia lost contact with the major and his Fourteenth Infantry Regiment on August 22, and the Japanese captured Nakar on September 29 and subsequently executed him in Manila.

On Panay, Filipino signal officers smuggled radio parts, generators, car and truck batteries, battery chargers, and gasoline out of Iloilo City. A radio came from a scuttled British oil tanker. After a two-month effort, signalmen coaxed the radio to life and decided to use the international radio guard frequency for ships in distress. The call went out, "Free Panay calling, Free Panay calling." For three days, there was no answer. Then station KKFS in San Francisco responded. But at that very moment Panay's radio broke down. It took ten days to find parts and get it working again. On October 30 Panay once again contacted San Francisco. The message to MacArthur read, in part:

We wish to report on the reorganization of the Visayas Free Forces into the IV Philippine Corps....Panay Island is fully reorganized into the 61st Division....Total men now on active service about eight thousand. Negros Island is being reorganized into the 83rd reorganized Division....

Mission being carried out by this corps is to maintain...independent loci of resistance in all islands pursuant to secret letter of in-

Poorly armed through most of the war, Filipino guerrillas were generally equipped with surviving American weapons or arms captured from the Japanese. Above: With a bolo at his waist, Ignacio Clero stands at shoulder arms. Opposite: An unidentified Filipino displays a variety of U.S. and Japanese equipment. His Pattern 1917 Enfield rifle and ammunition belt are U.S. issue; his field cap and Model 97 hand grenade are Japanese.

structions of MacArthur thru General Sharp sometime later part of December.

Badly need arms and ammunition caliber thirty. This is matter of life and death with us. In Panay we control the interior in general and most of the coastline. Planes can drop arms and ammunition in areas about five miles from capitals of provinces and can be sure of contacting us.

Civilians and officials about ninety percent loyal.

On November 5, the Panay forces received word that their message had reached MacArthur along with the wel-

come news that the guerrillas were still members of the armed forces of the United States. It was now up to the USAFFE commander to tighten these tenuous links and to gather the Filipino resistance movement into his military machine. In 1943 the task of doing just that devolved to the Philippine Regional Section. MacArthur called in a trusted adviser to run it, Colonel Courtney Whitney, a prominent Manila lawyer well versed in prewar conditions and the personalities of the Philippines. Whitney knew the islands from the fifteen years he had lived and worked there.

build organizations for covert operations and propaganda. MacArthur's headquarters came to rely on specially trained agents as well as established guerrilla units for intelligence about Japanese activities on the Philippines.

Instrumental in training Filipino agents, as well as establishing an intelligence network and communication links with Australia, was Major Jesus Antonio Villamor. Villamor, along with three other Filipino officers and two enlisted men, had voluntarily returned to the islands in late December 1942. In his report of the team's operations, the major stressed that his intelligence operation was separate from existing guerrilla operations:

I established this network principally with the idea that this net would be entirely independent of all intelligence nets previously established by the guerrillas, believing that in all probability you [MacArthur] could rely more on guerrilla intelligence activities for the present. I wanted to establish something that would really be underground and as secret as possible. For that reason, I took my time about it. I took as much as two months to train each individual man. I tried to impress on each man that after he left my place, he would be on his own and that no matter what happened to me or to the rest of the net, he would carry on. I assured him that both GHQ and I would have faith in him.

Villamor's network would eventually provide information on Japanese activities across Luzon and the Visayan Islands.

Establishing friendly relations with the established guerrilla groups was also of critical importance to U.S. headquarters, and Lt. Cmdr. Charles Parsons was tasked with making personal contact with the fighters. In March 1943, he arrived by submarine at Mindanao Island with a radio and supplies. MacArthur had given Parsons authority to officially recognize guerrilla leaders and arrange to send them aid. Recognition was critically important to these commanders—yet not every band should be recognized, for not all guerrilla leaders were effective. A few had made truces with the Japanese, and many knew nothing of the military, of leadership, or of staff work. Some others had become intoxicated with never-before-held power.

During a May 24, 1943, briefing, MacArthur tasked Whitney with organizing, supplying, and coordinating all Filipino guerrilla activity. The first priority was to establish communications and intelligence-gathering networks; the second priority was to counter Japanese propaganda; the third was to build guerrilla units capable of striking Japanese rear areas once American conventional troops arrived. General MacArthur stressed the guerrillas' first priority. Offensive operations this early would only expose the guerrilla organizations and bring reprisals down on civilians.

Collecting information would be difficult but not impossible. Guerrillas in the field could report on Japanese movements and troop dispositions. Hotel clerks could furnish guest lists and information about Japanese conferences. Dockworkers could count incoming and outgoing troops and supplies. Mechanics at airfields could track enemy aircraft. MacArthur, however, needed trained agents in order to expand and direct guerrilla activities. Agents were also needed to establish intelligence nets, install local communications and links to Australia, develop escape routes for important personages, and

Parsons had to ensure that each leader was loyal, capable, and willing to take orders. And these commanders had to have subordinates equally willing to submit to orders and discipline. More military advantage could be gained in an hour by one coastwatcher whose spotting led to a ship sinking than by a year of guerrillas taking potshots at individ-ual Japanese soldiers. Yet the average Filipino wanted immediate revenge against the Japanese invaders, not a sunken troopship. Parsons had to learn whether local leaders would support coastwatchers and refrain from serious attacks on garrisons.

The first guerrilla commander Parsons met with was Lt. Col. Wendell W. Fertig on Mindanao. A reservist, the American mining engineer had been called to active duty in 1941. He avoided the surrender and linked with a Philippine constabulary captain who was organizing guerrillas. Fertig's men had quickly liberated huge tracts of Mindanao.

Since December of 1942, the colonel had been blindly radioing Australia, using a code the army had suspended after Corregidor fell. San Francisco had heard these transmissions but feared Japanese trickery and ignored the messages. The frustrated colonel finally decided to send three American officers all the way to Australia in an open boat. In an astounding display of navigation and good luck, the men arrived safely, bearing a simple call-sign code so that Australia could communicate with Mindanao. Colonel Peralta, leader of the guerrillas on Panay Island, was also able to establish communications with Australia in early 1943. On February 21, MacArthur's headquarters radioed Fertig and Peralta to inform them of their appointments as commanders of the Tenth and the Sixth military districts, respectively.

Parsons, after meeting with Fertig and confirming his appointment, moved through the islands to Leyte—then on

During the occupation, supplies trickled in to the Filipino fighters via U.S. Navy submarines. After American forces returned to the Philippines in late 1944, however, food and equipment flowed in much more freely. Opposite: Sailors and Filipinos unload bags of rice at a guerrilla headquarters on Mindanao in May 1945. Above: Filipino guerrillas on Samar Island are issued newly arrived supplies.

to Panay, where he confirmed Peralta's appointment—then to Samar, Negros, and Cebu. Filipinos were tremendously happy to see this American, a representative from the revered MacArthur. Fresh American cigarettes and recent issues of *Time* magazine convinced them that Parsons actually did come from Australia. The same question met Parsons at every stop: "When will the aid come? When will MacArthur return and kick out the Japanese?"

Parsons' pitch in soliciting Filipino army officers to lead resistance groups was effective. On Leyte, Colonel Kangleon responded: "…this is not the time for an old soldier to rest. You have made my duty clear, Commander Parsons. I have no choice. You may tell General MacArthur I am ready to serve."

The U.S. Navy began using the submarines *Nautilus* and *Narwhal* for supply runs to the Philippines. Too big and clumsy to run normal anti-shipping patrols, the boats could be used for special missions, such as the insertion of supplies and spies. First seven tons, then thirty tons, then even more came ashore at secluded beaches. The supplies included arms, munitions, radios, generators, fuel to run the generators, genuine peso paper money, and medical supplies, as well as rifles for guerrillas desperate for weapons. Cigarettes and up-to-date magazines appeared, even at the most remote guerrilla hideout. As a result, the resisters' morale climbed, and after June 1943 MacArthur made more and more assets available to the Filipinos.

The guerrillas' communications network on Leyte in 1944 illustrates how intelligence was radioed to MacArthur. Guerrilla patrols used several contact stations to keep Colonel Kangleon's headquarters informed of Japanese activities. Kangleon, in turn, was in touch with MacArthur's headquarters. Two additional coastwatcher stations kept the USAFFE commander informed of Japanese ship movements or troop landings. Kangleon was also able to use one of these sets to keep in touch with Colonel Fertig on Mindanao. Between March and October 1944, General Headquarters in Australia received 101 messages from the guerrillas on Leyte.

U.S. submarines, however, could not ship supplies in fast enough, and many guerrillas did not receive any supplies until 1944 or not at all. According to Vicente Sydiongco: "Not until the early part of 1944 did we receive very limited arms and ammunition from the Southwest Pacific Area Command, shipped in by submarine. In fact, I know of only one such shipment for the Leyte guerrilla command." Another group, the U.S. Army Forces in the Philippines, Northern Luzon (USAFIP[NL]), numbered eight thousand guerrillas in January 1945, but only two thousand were well armed.

As guerrilla intelligence-gathering activities increased in 1943, Japanese authorities attempted to coax the rebels to surrender by offering them amnesty and jobs. Some Filipinos, including several subordinates of General Miranda, accepted the offer. But resistance continued, and Japan soon resorted to reinforcing its garrisons and aggressively hunting down the guerrillas. After the rebels retreated into the mountains, the Japanese launched large-scale conventional operations designed to destroy the civilian support base upon which the guerrillas depended. They used Filipino forced labor to harvest and transport crops, occupying interior towns and burning the remotest barrios they could find. It was frustrating work, since the Japanese could seldom bring the guerrillas to battle.

Confirmed kills and captured weapons were disappointingly small. Although unable to find many guerrillas, the Japanese had no trouble finding civilians. Murders, hangings, and mutilations followed the Japanese troops. A Filipino civil affairs officer on Panay reported to local guerrillas, "In barrio Napnapan alone, thirty-seven charred bodies were discovered; in barrio Bocari, the estimated dead is not less than fifty; in barrio Bagongbong, at least one hundred twenty were mercilessly butchered—men, women, and children."

The relentless pressure brought results. The respected governor of free Ilocos Norte Province, who had stirred up effective resistance across northwest Luzon, disappeared without a trace. In October 1942, the Japanese captured Colonel Claude Thorp, who had operated in the Mount Pinatubo area and controlled much of the central Luzon guerrilla movement. The Japanese broke up

Guerrillas were able to assist in the reconquest of the Philippines by providing arriving U.S. forces with intelligence on Japanese troop strengths and deployments. On Panay, Colonel Marcario Peralta and his guerrillas supplied newly landed troops of the 185th U.S. Infantry Regiment with information on Japanese troops in the area that facilitated the soldiers' advance later that day (above).

Colonel Hugh Straughn's east central Luzon guerrillas and captured Straughn. An eight-month anti-guerrilla campaign and the capture of two more American colonels in June 1943 sent the morale of north Luzon guerrillas to new lows. Japanese pressure had reduced those northern guerrilla forces by 70 percent, to about two thousand badly scattered men. Radio contact with Australia had been lost, and supplies of medicine and ammunition were exhausted.

In late May 1943, the Japanese poured troops into Mindanao and shattered guerrilla resistance on the island. Fertig wrote in his diary, "Unless a United States offensive starts very soon, we are lost, for we cannot meet the full force of the enemy." Gone now were electric lights, bustling barrios, and busy ports. Guerrilla-sponsored libraries, civilian relief projects, and volunteer guards all collapsed. The Japanese killed work animals, burned homes, and destroyed or stole crops. "We cannot keep this up

much longer," wrote a Filipino judge. "We cannot plant, *évacués* are dying of malaria in the forests, there are scarcely enough well to take care of the sick and dying. Our civilian government has broken down, and officials are fleeing from their posts. Our spirit is becoming broken by the length of the war."

Although Japanese brutalities failed to completely eliminate the guerrilla organizations, large numbers of guerrillas did run away. Others had so little training that when they fought, they inflicted little harm on the enemy. The hard-core Filipino rebels sniped, slipped away, and sniped again. Nothing they did, however, seriously slowed the big enemy columns. All they could do was lie low while the Japanese ravaged their lands.

Inhibited by their own weakness, the guerrillas remained true, by necessity and not choice, to their first priority—MacArthur's priority—that of maintaining their organizations. By refusing

conventional combat, the Filipinos prevented the Japanese from determining the size and significance of the resistance movement. Had the guerrillas fought, the Japanese would have reinforced their punitive columns and destroyed the poorly armed bands.

Unable to find the light-footed guerrillas with large columns, the Japanese columns were broken into smaller elements and sent farther and farther into unknown territory. Filipinos who had run from the large columns suddenly found themselves numerically superior to these detachments. The guerrillas bushwhacked the smallest and most careless patrols. This did not stop the Japanese, but it helped Filipino morale and showed the populace that supporting the guerrillas meant dead Japanese.

After nearly a year of scorched-earth operations, Japanese activities declined. More than ten thousand civilians had died on Panay alone. The Japanese had strengthened their garrisons. The guerrillas, although exhausted and poorly armed, had generally followed MacArthur's orders to save themselves for later operations. Yet they burned to strike back.

Despite occasional guerrilla losses, as well as terror tactics against civilians, the Japanese never convinced enough Filipinos that the United States might actually lose the war, and morale was generally good. Filipinos listened to hidden civilian radios and heard news of American progress in the Pacific. Newspapers and magazines brought in on American submarines circulated through hundreds of hands.

By 1944, two years of war, guerrilla operations, and Japanese reprisals had worn heavily on the Filipino people. More frequent than ever, anti-guerrilla operations were strongly manned and of increasing duration. The report of the Japanese commander on Leyte gives an idea of the scope of Japanese operations on the island from January 1 to August 31. He claimed that his troops had seized seven generators, thirty-seven radios, 1,556 weapons, and 55,348 rounds of ammunition, as well as sticks of dynamite. The offensive cut many Filipino lines of communication and supply. "It is very easy to evade the Japanese," wrote one commander, "but you cannot evade starvation."

At the same time, 1944 witnessed a substantial increase in the number of American submarine insertions. On one landing, sailors aboard *Narwhal* were astounded to find themselves at a concrete pier, with dockhands to handle mooring lines, trucks and launches to receive supplies, and the 110th Division's band in white shirts and trousers playing "Aloha" and "Stars and Stripes Forever."

"Jesus Christ!" a sailor exclaimed, "where the hell are we—Hollywood?" In turn, *Narwhal* stupefied the Filipinos by its huge size and the ninety tons of supplies it delivered. The submarine's arrival must have also been a welcome sight to the 110th's commander, Lt. Col. Paul H. Marshall, who had escaped from a Japanese POW camp in April 1943 and joined the guerrillas. Sixteen days later, *Narwhal* delivered another one hundred tons of materiel.

Resistance propaganda to counter similar Japanese efforts soon spread across the islands. Millions of packs of cigarettes, gum, candy, pencils, and sewing kits were imprinted with "I shall return. MacArthur" and delivered by sub. Large numbers of the publication *Free Philippines* came ashore, as did newspapers and periodicals. Not all of it was well received. Colonel Russell Volckmann, commander of the USAFIP(NL), was disappointed to receive several heavy boxes full of propaganda materials stamped "I shall return." He sent a message to headquarters discouraging further propaganda supplies and asked for weapons and ammunition instead. He then developed a motto for his guerrillas: We Remained.

On October 20, 1944, MacArthur finally did return to the Philippines, as U.S. troops landed on Leyte. Three days later at a ceremony restoring the Philippine civilian government, guerrilla leader Colonel

'It is very easy to evade the Japanese,' wrote one commander, 'but you cannot evade starvation.'

Kangleon was awarded the Distinguished Service Cross. At that time there were 134 guerrilla-supported radio stations and twenty-three weather stations operating in the Philippines.

The guerrillas on Leyte, and on Luzon after U.S. troops landed there in January 1945, could finally go on the offensive, and the resistance fighters' ranks swelled. According to the U.S. Army's official history of World War II, the presence of the large, organized Filipino guerrilla force "waiting to make its contribution to the defeat of Japan" was a phenomenon "certainly far different from any other experience of the war in the Pacific." The guerrillas often served as scouts for U.S. units and were able to pinpoint enemy positions, as well as their arms and fuel depots. Filipino patrols harassed enemy troops, especially detached elements and men and vehicles on the march. Resistance units carried out ambushes, night operations, sabotage, and demolitions as well as rear-guard duties for U.S. combat units.

Undoubtedly the guerrillas were driven by a desire for revenge and eager to finally fight back. American troops were often shocked by the ruthlessness of the resistance fighters. Buck Creel, executive officer of a company in the U.S. Ninety-sixth Infantry Division, recounted one incident in which three Filipinos wishing to become scouts were tasked with eliminating some Japanese soldiers:

About dusk the following day, the trio came trotting back into the defensive perimeter....I noticed one guerrilla had a rice-straw bag over his shoulder. Upon a nod from the head honcho, he shook it out and five Japanese heads tumbled out at my feet....Needless to say, our newfound "Scouts" were welcomed into G Company and spent the rest of the campaign as an integral part of our unit.

Some guerrilla units were able to serve as regular combat forces. Two months after the invasion of Luzon, the size of Colonel Volckmann's USAFIP(NL) had grown to eighteen thousand guerrillas. Their role in the fighting gradually enlarged to the point that they were substituted for U.S. divisions and were a key component in the army's liberation of northern Luzon. During 1945, the guerrilla unit was directly or indirectly responsible for the deaths of about ten thousand Japanese soldiers and sustained roughly thirty-four hundred casualties.

The end of the war found twenty-one thousand Filipino guerrillas fighting in northern Luzon alone. Another twenty-two thousand Filipinos operated elsewhere on Luzon. In the southern islands, about seventy-five thousand men and women were in the field. These totals, although possibly inflated, were higher than the conventional Filipino army MacArthur had mobilized in late 1941.

Filipinos had faced three years of Japanese oppression, and they had kept the faith. America's forty years of rule had established such a reservoir of goodwill and trust that nothing the Japanese did, either with blandishments or force, could turn the Filipinos from their allegiance to the United States or from their belief in themselves.

John W. Whitman is the author of *Bataan: Our Last Ditch, The Bataan Campaign, 1942* (Hippocrene Books, 1990).

British Observers

Four British visitors recorded memorable observations of the South's leaders as well as its common folk during trips that spanned the life of the Confederacy.

by John M. Taylor

When the states of the lower South began seceding from the Union at the end of 1860, the editors of the London *Times* could see that this was a fairly big story, one perhaps calling for a special correspondent. And because the unrest in America might even lead to war, they looked for someone with military qualifications. Their choice fell on stocky, brown-bearded William Howell Russell, who had reported on the Crimean War for the *Times*. He would be the first of at least four prominent British correspondents whose business, or interests, took them to the wartime Confederacy on different missions at different times.

Some of these transatlantic reporters started in the North. Russell reached New York in March 1861, shortly after Abraham Lincoln's inauguration, and made his way to Washington. There, he met all the right people and concluded, in one of his more astute appraisals, that the gangling new president was not the "incompetent gorilla" that some made him out to be. But Russell's main interest was the South, which, after all, was where the story was. So after several weeks in Washington, he set out for Virginia by way of a steamer from Baltimore to Norfolk.

Russell's first impressions of the South were not favorable. He found Norfolk's Atlantic Hotel "a dilapidated, uncleanly place, with tobacco-stained floor, full of flies." Nor was he impressed with Southern speech. But he was interested in the physical appearance of his first Southerners, whom he found to be "of a new and marked type, very tall, loosely yet powerfully made." They might make good fighters.

Russell's immediate goal was Charleston, South Carolina, and he traveled there by train. Although the upper South states of Virginia and North Carolina had not yet seceded, everywhere along the way he found the people ecstatic over the recent surrender of Fort Sumter. He wrote of his stop at Goldsboro, North Carolina, "The station, the hotels, the street through which the rail ran was filled with an excited mob, all carrying arms, with signs here and there of a desire to get up some kind of uniform—flushed faces, wild eyes, screaming mouths, hurrahing for 'Jeff Davis' and 'the Southern Confederacy,' so that the yells overpowered the discordant bands which were busy with 'Dixie's Land.'"

Left: London Times *reporter William Howell Russell got a firsthand look at slavery. Inset left: Garnet J. Wolseley thought Robert E. Lee "a splendid specimen of an English gentleman." Above: Irishman Thomas Conolly was one of the Confederacy's final foreign visitors. No known image exists of Arthur J.L. Fremantle, who viewed the Battle of Gettysburg.*

At Charleston, Russell met with General P.G.T. Beauregard, the "victor of Sumter," who treated him with the courtesy to which British visitors to the Confederacy would become accustomed. On April 19 the Creole general told Russell that much depended on Virginia, which he viewed as slow to act following Lincoln's call for troops with which to put down the rebellion. At one dinner, Russell met a member of a prominent Charleston family, the Hugers. Tears rolled down the cheeks of the paterfamilias when he spoke of the possibility of civil war, but according to Russell, "there was no symptom of apprehension for the result, or, indeed, of any regret for the contest, which he regarded as the natural consequence of the insults, injustice, and aggression of the North against Southern rights."

Like many visitors to the South, Russell was eager to see slavery firsthand, and to hear the slave owners' explanations of the institution. In Charleston, he stayed at the home of William Trescott, who had served as acting secretary of state under President James Buchanan. Russell noted the squalor of the Trescotts' slave quarters, but was impressed that Mrs. Trescott spent much of one night nursing a sick servant.

The British visitor moved on to Savannah in early May, where he attended his first slave auction, held just outside his hotel, and acknowledged himself "much affected." The auctioneer appeared to Russell "an ill-favored, dissipated-looking rascal," while the bidders and onlookers were a "listless gathering of men…whittling and chewing." The single male slave to be sold that day was "a

stout young Negro, badly dressed and ill shod." Russell provided a vivid picture of the occasion:

A man in a cart, some volunteers in coarse uniform, a few Irish laborers…and four or five men in the usual black coat, satin waistcoat, and black hat, constituted the audience, whom the auctioneer addressed volubly: "A prime field hand! Just look at him—good-natured, well-tempered; no marks, nary sign of bad about him! En-i-ne hundred—only nine hundred and fifty dol'rs for 'em! Why it's quite rad-aklous! Nine hundred and fifty dol'rs! I can't raly—That's good. Thank you, sir. Twenty-five bid—nine hun-therd and seventy-five dol'rs for this most useful hand." The price rose to one thousand dollars, at which the useful hand was knocked down to one of the black hats near me.

On May 9, Russell took a coastal steamer, *Southern Republic*, for the four-hundred-mile voyage from Savannah around Florida to Mobile, Alabama. There he met two colonels, Dabney Maury and William Hardee, soon to become prominent general officers, and was able to visit Fort Pickens, Florida, which was still in Union hands. Russell was impressed with the defensive potential of Forts Gaines and Morgan at the entrance to Mobile Bay, but concluded that much would depend on the quality of their garrisons.

From Mobile, Russell traveled to New Orleans and then to Baton Rouge. It was June by then. The Federals had proclaimed a blockade of Southern ports, and Russell wondered whether any of his dispatches to the *Times* were getting through. Concluding that it was time to return to the North and its more reliable communications, Russell took a riverboat up the Mississippi to Memphis, where he called on the local Confederate commander, General Gideon Pillow. Russell knew enough of military matters to be skeptical of Pillow's river defenses, and his doubts were underscored when he observed some target practice along the Mississippi:

The General ordered some practice to be made with round shot down the river. An old forty-two pound carronade was loaded with some difficulty, and pointed at a tree about 1,700 yards…distant. The General and his staff took their posts on the parapet to the leeward, and I ventured to say, "I think, General, the smoke will prevent your seeing the shot." To which the General replied, "No, sir," in a tone which indicated, "I beg you to understand I have been wounded in Mexico, and know all about this kind of thing."

According to Russell, the gun was eventually fired, "but where the ball went, no one could say, as the smoke drifted right into our eyes."

With Pillow's blessing, Russell crossed back into the North at Cairo, Illinois. The reporter made his way east, arriving in Washington just in time to report on the Federal rout at the First Battle of Bull Run in such caustic prose that he would be known thereafter as "Bull Run" Russell. He hung around Washington for another eight months, but when he was refused permission to accompany Maj. Gen. George B. McClellan on his 1862 Peninsula campaign, Russell realized that his usefulness as a reporter was over. He went back to Britain in 1862, never to return.

Today Russell is better remembered for his coverage of First Bull Run than for his earlier dispatches from the South. The latter, however, were insightful, even when eventually proved faulty. He erred, for instance, in his belief that the Union could not be restored by force, that even a Northern victory "must destroy the Union as it has been constituted in the past." At the same time, Russell recognized that Southerners were far too dismissive of the North. Everything he had seen in the Confederacy, he wrote, "testifies to the great zeal and resolution with which the South have entered upon the quarrel. But they hold the power of the United States and the loyalty of the North to the Union at far too cheap a rate." Not a bad observation considering it was made in June 1861.

The first British soldier to visit the Confederacy had at one time expected to be fighting against the North. Lieutenant Colonel Garnet J. Wolseley, a veteran of several of Queen Victoria's wars, was part of a British force ordered to Canada in 1861 as a show of strength after the U.S. Navy stopped the British mail packet *Trent* and seized two Confederate agents who were on board. The threat of war receded, however, and Wolseley found himself with time on his hands. Taking two months' leave, he traveled from Canada to New York City in September 1862. There he joined forces with Frank Lawley, William Howard Russell's successor as correspondent for the London *Times*, to visit the Confederacy. By the time the two men crossed the Potomac, General Robert E. Lee's army was withdrawing from Maryland at the conclusion of the Antietam campaign.

Even as he entered Virginia, Wolseley was favorably disposed toward the Confederacy, ostensibly out of concern for civil liberties in the wartime North. He described residents of Maryland as "stricken…with terror" by arrests ordered from Washington. In the one article he wrote while the war was in progress, Wolseley would decline to describe his route through Maryland, lest he endanger those with whom he had stayed.

Traveling by train from Fredericksburg to Richmond, Wolseley and Lawley shared accommodations with the wounded from Lee's Maryland invasion. Their plight impressed even Wolseley, the professional soldier:

Men with legs and arms amputated, and whose pale, haggard faces assumed an expression of anguish at even the slightest jolting of the railway carriages, lay stretched across the seats—some accompanied by civilian friends who had gone from Richmond to the front to fetch them back, and others by wives or sisters, whose careworn features told a tale of sleepless nights passed in painful uncertainty regarding the fate of those they loved.

At Richmond, Wolseley found accommodations at one of the lesser hotels, the Exchange. He observed that prices were high, with tea selling at sixteen dollars per pound. Liquor was hard to come by because the government had banned its production, a prohibition that Wolseley thought was wise. "Few men are fonder of spirits than the Southerners," he would write. "If the sale of spirits had been allowed, I feel convinced that it would not only have been impossible to keep order, but that the great things which have been effected by their armies would not have been achieved."

Richmond provided Wolseley with his first look at the institution of slavery. His perspective was one of curiosity rather than reproach:

When a man talks of his servants in the South, he is always understood to mean his slaves. It is for this reason that in the North no white man is ever called a servant; the term *help* being used instead. All the hotels and establishments requiring a large number of hands have slaves hired from masters, who let them out precisely in the same manner that a livery-stable keeper in England lets out his horses.

From Richmond, Wolseley made day trips to various locations, and he appears to have had a free run of military installations. He was impressed with the defensive works on Drewry's Bluff, overlooking the James River, and with Confederate efforts at shipbuilding. "An indolent race," he wrote of the Southerners, "who, before the commencement of hostilities, despised all manual labour, and thought only of amusement…have now shown that when a necessity for exertion arises, they not only do not shrink from it, but meet it nobly."

In early October, Wolseley set out for Lee's headquarters, then near Culpeper Court House. His driver was a convalescent soldier who was still in considerable discomfort. When Wolseley asked why he didn't stay at home longer, "He said that his furlough was up, and he would rather die than overstay it….Indifferent to his own comforts as this man was, yet, when spoken to about the war, he would change in a moment—he, and every man in the South, were prepared to die, he said, but never to reunite with the d—d Yankees."

When Wolseley reached the Army of Northern Virginia's headquarters, he and a traveling companion, who may have been Lawley, presented letters of introduction to Lee's staff and were taken to meet the general. The British officer was impressed:

[Lee] is a strongly built man, about five feet eleven in height, and apparently not more than fifty years of age [Lee was 55]. His hair and beard are nearly white; but his dark brown eyes still shine with all the brightness of youth, and beam a most pleasing expression....He is slightly reserved; but he is a person that, wherever seen, whether in a castle or a hovel, alone or in a crowd, must at once attract attention as being a splendid specimen of an English gentleman.

Wolseley found an appealing lack of pomp and ostentation at Lee's headquarters, which, he noted, consisted of seven or eight pole tents, pitched on ground so rocky as to be uncomfortable to ride over. Lee's staff lived two or three to each tent, a nearby stream the only amenity. A few horses roamed in an adjacent field, but no guards or sentries were in evidence. Everywhere he was impressed with the tough, dedicated Confederate soldiers. Could such men be defeated, he would ask, "by mobs of Irish and German mercenaries, hired at $15 a month to fight in a cause they know little and care less about?"

Lee put a wagon at the disposal of his visitors, who chose to ride to the nearby camp of the famous Thomas J. "Stonewall" Jackson. Wolseley did not warm to Jackson as he had to Lee, but would write that Jackson's "thin compressed lips and calm glance" were evidence of the "firmness and decision of character" for which he was noted.

Wolseley had arrived in Virginia with a bias against the North; he left it a month later a strong advocate for the South. On his return to Britain, he wrote an article for *Blackwood's Magazine* titled "A Month's Visit to the Confederate Headquarters," and it is from this piece—Wolseley's only writing contemporary to the Civil War—that quotations have been taken. At the close of his article, Wolseley urged the British Parliament to intervene on behalf of the South, saying that the time had come "for putting an end to the most inhuman struggle that ever disgraced a great nation."

Wolseley went on to a prominent career in the British army, distinguishing himself in the 1873-74 Second Ashanti War and becoming a favorite of Prime Minister Benjamin Disraeli's. He led the relief expedition in 1884 that attempted unsuccessfully to rescue General Charles Gordon from besieging dervishes in Khartoum. Although Wolseley was severely criticized for the deliberate pace of his advance, and for the resulting death of

Gordon, he was promoted to field marshal in 1894.

Wolseley never lost his interest in the American Civil War and wrote extensively on the subject for periodicals on both sides of the Atlantic. Something of a military reformer, Wolseley believed that there was much to be learned from America's war. He studied Grant's use of railroads and early amphibious efforts, such as the U.S. Navy's operations against Charleston, South Carolina.

Wolseley also retained his admiration for Robert E. Lee. In an article written for *McMillan's* in 1887, he wrote, "I have met but two men who realize my ideas of what a true hero should be: my friend Charles Gordon was one, General Lee was the other."

The best-known narrative by a visitor to the Confederacy is that of Lt. Col. Arthur J.L. Fremantle, who visited the wartime South for three months in the spring and early summer of 1863. Fremantle not only spent more time in the Confederacy than the others here considered, but his timing was the best. After traveling through the lower South from his entry point in Texas, Fremantle reached Richmond when the Confederate star was at its zenith. He caught up with Lee's army in time for the Gettysburg campaign, and his account of that battle is one of the most riveting to come out of the war.

In Charleston, Fremantle heard of a slave auction scheduled for that day. The Englishman arrived after the sale, and his comments on it were notably bland. He described the newly sold slaves, nearly twenty in all, as "looking perfectly contented and indifferent," even as their new buyers required them to show their teeth as evidence of good health. Fremantle found this "not a very agreeable spectacle to an Englishman," but went on to speculate that if the Southern states were left alone, the system of slavery "would be much modified and amended, although complete emancipation cannot be expected."

In Richmond, Fremantle had the same ready access to Confederate leaders that Russell and Wolseley had enjoyed. He found President Jefferson Davis looking old and worn, but insisted that nothing could exceed the charm of his manner,

"which is simple, easy, and most fascinating." The Englishman had a lengthy discussion with Secretary of State Judah P. Benjamin, whom Fremantle described as "a stout, dapper little man, evidently of Hebrew extraction, and of undoubted talent." The two discussed the legitimacy of secession, which Benjamin defended with vigor.

In Richmond, Fremantle fell in with Garnet Wolseley's friend Francis Lawley of the London Times and, having been briefed on Lee's forthcoming campaign in Pennsylvania, set out to find the Army of Northern Virginia. Although travel was difficult and Lawley was ill, the two caught up with Lt. Gen. James Longstreet's corps at Chambersburg, Pennsylvania, on June 27. Like Russell and Wolseley, Fremantle was impressed with the Confederate fighters. He left a memorable description of Maj. Gen. John B. Hood's troops, which would play so prominent a role on the second day of the coming battle: "This division, well known for its fighting qualities, is composed of Texans, Alabamians, and Arkansans, and they certainly are a queer lot to look at. They carry less than any other troops; many of them have only got an old piece of carpet or rug as baggage; many have discarded their shoes in the mud; all are ragged and dirty, but full of good humor and confidence in themselves and their general, Hood."

Fremantle had letters of introduction to Longstreet and quickly made himself at home at First Corps headquarters. One of the general's aides described Fremantle as "a very small, slight man, wiry, and much enduring." Historical novelist Michael Shaara, in *The Killer Angels*, portrays the British colonel as "a scrawny man, toothy, with a pipelike neck and monstrous Adam's apple. He looked like a popeyed bird who had just swallowed something large and sticky and triangular." The Englishman's appearance was quixotic to say the least, and he doubtless was the butt of some heavy-handed Rebel humor.

On June 30, the day before the Battle of Gettysburg began, Longstreet introduced Fremantle to Robert E. Lee. Fremantle later wrote: "He is fifty-six years old, tall, broad-shouldered, very well made...a thorough soldier in appearance; and his manners are most courteous and full of dignity. He is a perfect gentleman in every respect. I imagine no man [in the South] has so few enemies, or is so universally esteemed."

Lee, at that time, was a troubled commander. He had little intelligence regarding the approaching Yankee army and was on the brink of the greatest disaster that would befall the Army of Northern Virginia. But no hint of Lee's troubles emerged in his conversation with Fremantle, who was encouraged to observe what became the greatest battle of the war.

On July 2, the crucial second day of the battle, Fremantle shared a tree near Lee's headquarters with Lawley of the *Times* and a Prussian observer, Justus Scheibert. Fremantle is the source of the charge that Lee was largely detached from the events of that day, sending only one message and receiving only one report.

It was Fremantle who accompanied Lee to Longstreet's front on July 3, after the disaster of Pickett's Charge. In the Englishman's memorable description:

[Lee's] face, which is always placid and cheerful, did not show signs of the slightest disappointment, care, or annoyance; and he was addressing to every soldier he met a few words of encouragement....He spoke to all the wounded men that passed him, and the slightly wounded he exhorted "to bind up their hurts and take up a musket" in this emergency. Very few failed to answer his appeal, and I saw many badly wounded men take off their hats and cheer him. He said to me, "This has been a sad day for us, Colonel—a sad day; but we can't expect always to gain victories."

After Gettysburg, Fremantle made his way through the Federal lines and returned to England. Like Wolseley, he was eager to be of assistance to the Confederacy and wrote an account of the Gettysburg campaign for the same conservative journal for which Wolseley had written, *Blackwood's Magazine*. This was followed in autumn 1863 by his full account, *Three Months in the Southern States: April–June, 1863*. The book was reprinted in both the North and the South, but it was especially appreciated by Southerners for its friendly tone.

Like Wolseley, Fremantle went on to a distinguished career in his own army,

gaining the rank of general and serving for four years as governor of Malta. Yet he is best known for having written the most vivid account of the Civil War by a foreign visitor.

Perhaps the last foreign visitor to the Confederacy—he arrived just in time to witness its collapse—was the strangest of all. Thomas Conolly, forty-one, was a member of the British Parliament and the master of a stately home in County Kildare, Ireland. Although a partisan of the South, his visit to the Confederacy was prompted by commercial considerations. Conolly had fallen on hard times. His estate was encumbered, and he needed money. Ever optimistic, and oblivious to the declining fortunes of the Confederacy, Conolly saw a voyage through the Federal blockade as his financial salvation.

In the autumn of 1864, he and several associates purchased a blockade runner, *Emily*, with which they hoped to exchange a cargo of general merchandise for precious Southern cotton. On December 7, 1864, *Emily* sailed from Cardiff, Wales, with Conolly and three of his partners on board. When the ship was damaged in a storm and had to turn back to the Madeira Islands, Conolly chose to continue in another vessel. After twelve days of revelry in Funchal, Conolly and one of his partners took passage on *Florence* to the Bahamas.

By the time they reached Nassau, the Confederacy was in its last throes. Atlanta had fallen, Richmond was besieged, and the Confederacy was running out of ports. At this point, Conolly may have been more in search of adventure than profits. In Nassau, he met John N. Maffitt, who had gained fame as skipper of the Confederate cruiser *Florida*, and who in 1865 was still active as a blockade runner. In February 1865, Maffitt was planning a final run through the blockade, and he agreed to land Conolly somewhere along the Carolina coast.

When Conolly disembarked some thirty-five miles south of Wilmington, North Carolina, he may have wished himself back in Nassau. He wrote in his diary on February 26: "Very cold night & no covering got me up by 4:00 & find we had made 8 fathoms sounding & were standing on & off waiting for light to

make our destination. At daylight, saw the loom of the land thro' thick mist tho' it was 9 o'clock before we could see it distinctly....We hugged the shore till 10:30, when we cast anchor opposite to Shallotte bar."

Conolly and two companions made their way north through "the unvaried pine forest," sometimes wading through knee-deep water. The inhabited areas he saw were not impressive. Conolly wrote on February 28 that "plantations are miserable enough & few & far between," a typical one consisting of "a wooden house raised on piles with 3 or 4 slave cottages, barn &c. &c. a miserable cow & horse tethered & the well in front with its long balance pole & bucket." Conolly was not especially interested in the Southerners whom he met along the way. Near Greensboro, North Carolina, he was served "a most wretched breakfast close to Railway & when I told the Lady presiding my opinion of it she flouted out in high dudgeon."

Conolly and his friends arrived at Richmond by way of Danville, Virginia, on March 8. The Irishman was impressed with the capital's physical setting but found it lacking in amenities. "The aspect of Richmond at this time is wretched," he wrote. "Shops with nothing in them except enough to show how miserably they are run out." He found rooms at the Ballard House and soon gained a reputation for high living. He noted that brandy was eighty dollars per bottle, but added, "We now have a...well organized bar & Henry our nigger is a proficient at the art of cocktails wh[ich] are served at first light every morning!"

Even as Confederate hopes faded, Conolly found a warm, official welcome. Five days after his arrival, he was invited to dinner by the president, and later wrote: "President Davis is a very remarkable man! His quiet manner & ready easy conversation with his clearly chiseled...face & grey eye & thin lips [and] aquiline nose mask a man of extraordinary determination....He makes a series of slight bows with his head when stating any proposition & is in all respects a graceful, spirited gentleman."

Conolly was such an uncritical Confederate supporter that he seized upon any military display by his hosts as grounds for optimism. In late March, he visited Drewry's Bluff, below which a rag-tag collection of gunboats, commanded by Raphael Semmes, sought to keep the Federal navy at bay. Conolly wrote in his diary how Semmes conducted him to a large barge, which he used as an office, and showed him around the gunboat that passed as his flagship, where Conolly had a "long talk with officers in Ward Room wh[ich] was headed by Semmes declaring he could not hope for intervention, but was sure the Confederacy could & would fight it out to a success!" If Conolly entertained any doubts with respect to Semmes' optimism, he did not confide them to his diary.

Conolly visited Lee's head-quarters on at least two occasions and was as taken with the commander as previous British visitors had been. The Irishman found the general a "most genial [and] kind man." Lee showed Conolly a map of Richmond's defenses at their first meeting and later urged his visitor to read the memoirs of Lee's old mentor, General Winfield Scott, of whom the Confederate general still spoke warmly.

Conolly, a Protestant, was in the congregation of St. Paul's Church on April 2 when word arrived that Union troops had broken Lee's lines and that the government must evacuate Richmond. "The sexton having stealthily whispered to Jeff. Davis," Conolly wrote, "he rises & leaves the [church]....People begin to whisper, [then] as if curiosity long suppressed had been ignited they rose (the whole congregation) in tens and 20s & left the Church." The visitor left a stark picture of the collapse of order as explosions racked the city. "There is the death knell of Richmond," he wrote. "...I went out & what a sight at that hour the streets filled with all the ragamuffins... running & hurrying about & then another crash another explosion & all the windows of the Spotswood [Hotel] are rent asunder as also [are] all the stores in Main Street. Now the plundering begins, men & women grabbing more than they can carry & bustling on...."

Conolly might have stayed in Richmond and counted on his status as a member of Parliament for protection. Instead, he left the city on foot with one or two companions. Conolly worked his way northeastward to Fredericksburg. Remarkably, he found a silver lining in the Confederates' debacle. Echoing Jefferson Davis, Conolly wrote in his diary on April 7, "The Confeds, altho they have

THE CIVIL WAR IN AMERICA: CAPTURE OF A UNITED STATES' DRAGOON BY GUERRILLA HORSEMEN OF VIRGINIA.—FROM A SKETCH BY OUR SPECIAL ARTIST.—SEE PAGE

The American Civil War captivated the British public as well as the press, as indicated by this front-page illustration depicting an early-war cavalry engagement. After their Southern sojourns, Wolseley and Fremantle recounted their observations for the conservative journal Blackwood's Magazine.

lost their far-famed city & Capital, have no longer 36 miles of works to defend but have the long wished for opportunity of meeting their deadly foe in the Field." But two days later, General Lee met his foe in the parlor of the McLean house at Appomattox.

As for Conolly, his luck held. Low on money, he worked as a deckhand on a vessel that took him up the Chesapeake Bay to Baltimore. From there, he traveled to New York, where he took passage home.

These four British visitors to the Confederacy varied widely in their objectivity and powers of observation. The most unbiased of the four clearly was Russell, who recognized before a shot had been fired that the South, as well as the North, was in for much more than it had anticipated. The least objective was Conolly, who as late as 1865 had little appreciation that the war was not going well for the Confederacy.

None of the four rubbed shoulders with a broad cross section of Southern society. In part because of the difficulties of travel, the Britons had little opportunity—Fremantle, perhaps, excepted—to study morale in the Confederate hinterland. Instead, they were wined and dined by senior officials and generals, all of whom were eager to cultivate foreign visitors. Except for references to inflation in Richmond, none of the four suggested in his writings that the Confederacy faced serious economic shortages and popular disenchantment with the war.

The two soldiers, Wolseley and Fremantle, appear to have been genuinely impressed with what they saw of the Army of Northern Virginia. Both seem to have been captivated by Robert E. Lee and easily won over to his cause. Although the ragtag Confederate army had little in common with Wolseley's and Fremantle's elite British regiments, the two soldiers were professional enough to recognize good fighters when they saw them. And in contrast to Russell, they were also willing to serve as witting propagandists for the Confederate cause.

All of the visitors except Conolly expressed some degree of distaste for the institution of slavery. But the two soldiers most easily accepted the rationalizations for slavery, perhaps because these were expressed by Southerners who seemed so like English gentlemen.

JOHN M. TAYLOR is the author of numerous books, including *Duty Faithfully Performed: Robert E. Lee and His Critics* (Brassey's, 1996).

Sir John Monash used his creative imagination and training as an engineer to achieve victories while leading the Australian Corps on the Western Front.

MONASH'S MASTERLY TOUCH

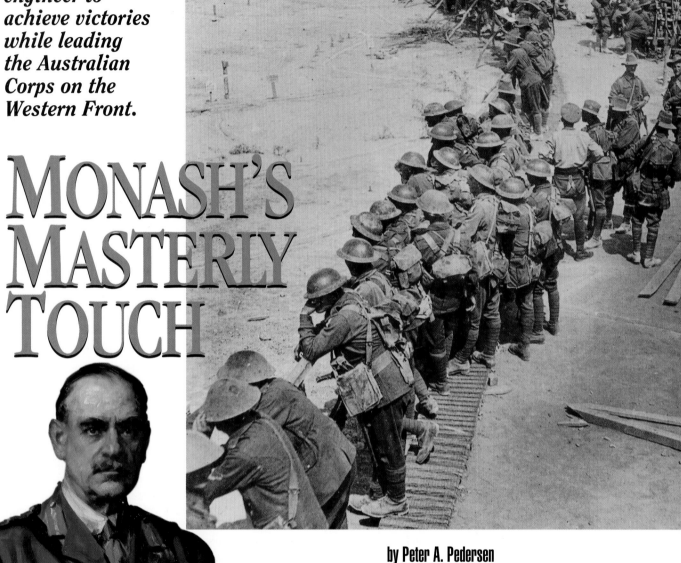

by Peter A. Pedersen

"If only the Generals had not been content to fight machine gun bullets with the breasts of gallant men, and think that that was waging war." Winston Churchill's despairing lament on World War I generalship still endures. Missing from the headstones in that graveyard of military reputations is the name of an Australian, General Sir John Monash. Under his leadership, the Australian Corps, which formed 9 percent of the British Expeditionary Force (BEF) in 1918, was responsible for capturing 22 percent of the prisoners and materiel seized by the BEF in the final months of the war. Field Marshal Bernard L. Montgomery and renowned military historian Sir Basil Liddell Hart were among those who considered Monash the best general on the Western Front.

Monash consistently demonstrated a formidable intellectual capacity. The future commander was born in Melbourne, Victoria, on June 27, 1865, to Jewish parents from Prussian Poland. Fluent in German, he graduated from

Melbourne University with degrees in engineering, arts, and law and became an engineer. Monash's intellect was matched by his vision. After seeing the latest technological advances during a long world tour in 1910, Monash bemoaned the inability of many of his countrymen to think on the grand scale and their reluctance to grasp the potential of a new idea. He went on to become one of the pioneers of reinforced concrete construction in Australia. In 1911 he supervised the building of Janvale Bridge, which boasted the largest spans in the country for a structure of its class.

Bridge building and other major engineering works gave Monash experience with large-scale engineering enterprises. Like the planning and execution of the big Western Front offensives, they required organization, direction, labor, and assembly and maintenance of resources. Moreover, the principles guiding the engineer—foresight, flexibility, co-operation, economy, delegation of authority, and an awareness of time—were equally applicable to high command. Drawing these comparisons after the war, Monash reflected that a background such as his was "far more useful for general applications to new problems than the comparatively narrow training of the professional soldier." Indeed, he never advocated the army as a career.

By 1914 Monash was a wealthy man, but his success did not come easily. He had often worked for expenses only and in remote parts of Australia, in the hope of winning lucrative future contracts. They rarely materialized, leaving Monash humiliated by indebtedness and hounded by creditors while he battled to support his wife and daughter. His health suffered, and he occasionally surrendered to fits of depression. Such personal adversities were akin to what Clausewitz called "the frictions" that were experienced at every level of wartime command. Overcoming them developed robustness in

Monash, "the ability to withstand the shocks of war" that the great soldier-scholar Field Marshal Archibald Wavell put at the top of his list of qualities a successful general must have.

Monash's thirty years of militia service was more serene. Much of it was with a technical arm, the Garrison Artillery. The intimate relationship between technology, the development of modern weapons, and the changes they wrought on warfare fascinated him. "Fighting Machinery," he concluded, had replaced physical force and brute courage. On a more mundane level, Monash responded

During the breakout from Anzac Cove in August 1915, Monash learned the limits to which men could be pushed.

to the outlook, aspirations, and needs of the soldiers in his battery with a leadership style based on concern for their welfare, quiet optimism, and a thorough knowledge of his responsibilities.

In March 1908, Monash took command of the Victorian section of the fledgling Australian Intelligence Corps. Really a surrogate Australian general staff, the corps prepared mobilization and interstate troop-movement plans, which Monash regarded primarily as logistical problems. He thought of logistics as an operation of war in an age when that term applied exclusively to combat, stating, "The task of bringing the force to the fighting point, properly equipped and well-formed in all that it needs is at least as important as the capable leading of the force in the fight itself."

As each plan took shape, Monash's ability to conceive it unfolding was often evident. Similarly, he could visualize the shape of terrain from the map depicting it. This power of creative imagination would be a priceless asset on the Western Front, where the scale of operations precluded commanders directing them from a single vantage point.

Monash's last prewar militia appointment was as commander of the Thirteenth Infantry Brigade. A trinity that he constantly espoused underpinned the brigade's training: unity of thought, of policy, and of tactical method. Monash would make the same appeal in every formation he subsequently led, and it formed the basis for discipline in them. Watching the Thirteenth Brigade on maneuvers in Australia in February 1914, General Sir Ian Hamilton, the inspector-general of British Overseas Forces, was struck by its enthusiasm and by Monash's technical proficiency and personal drive.

The pair next met in May 1915 on the Gallipoli Peninsula, where Hamilton commanded the Mediterranean Expeditionary Force and Monash's Fourth Australian Brigade clung desperately to the head of Monash Valley, which formed the most vulnerable part of the Anzac sector. The opposing trenches there were separated at one point only by a bombstop, and the Turks would have had an unimpeded passage to the nearby beach at Anzac Cove if they broke through his lines. Monash knew that holding the forward line in strength would be costly. His solution, praised as "an object lesson in covering fire," was to use well-sited machine guns to reduce the number of men needed along the front line, and to frequently relieve those soldiers in order to keep them fresh. The Australian official historian, C.E.W. Bean, later called the Fourth Brigade's five-week defense of Monash Valley one of the finest Australian feats of the war.

At Anzac Cove, Monash experienced the soldiers' war firsthand because the cramped conditions at the beachhead meant that headquarters were virtually in the front line. And as his exhausted brigade, wracked by dysentery and fever, responded to call after call during the breakout from Anzac in August 1915, he learned the limits to which men could be pushed. Perhaps he learned his own limitations, as well. Though robust enough for the sedentary battle in Monash Valley, at fifty he was too old for brigade command in the mobile operations that followed.

The August offensive was a failure, ending any chance of an Allied victory on Gallipoli. Its final operations, to link up with the British at Suvla, remain a delight for connoisseurs of military incompetence. Monash was powerless to intervene when his divisional commander changed the plan just before an attack, with predictable results for the Fourth Brigade, now less than nine hundred strong. From then on, Monash adopted Napoleon's aphorism: "Order, counterorder, disorder," and insisted that once issued, orders should not be modified unless "absolutely necessary for the safe conduct of the operation and the men."

On the Western Front, Monash commanded the Third Australian Division during the British Second Army's attacks on Messines Ridge in June 1917, and Broodseinde and Passchendaele in October during the Third Ypres offensive. Before Messines, he remarked that "Everything is being done with the perfection of a civil engineering construction so far as regards planning and execution." Every aspect of the Third Division's attack was covered in thirty-six separate instructions, while its preliminary bombardment program listed 446 targets. Monash then ran through the operation at a conference attended by commanders and staffs down to battalion level.

Messines and Broodseinde were smashing successes, largely because the objectives were shallow, so the assaulting infantry could reach them in sufficient strength to defeat the inevitable German counterattacks. The lesson was not lost on Monash, who had hitherto thought a modern, well-prepared defense virtually impregnable and had proved the point himself in Monash Valley. But by setting limited objectives, he now maintained: "So long as we hold and retain the initiative, we can in this way inflict the maximum of losses when and where we like. It restores to the offensive the advantages which are natural to the defensive in an unlimited objective."

Unfortunately, the objectives for Passchendaele were the deepest since the offensive began, the defending forces were infinitely stronger than those at Broodseinde, and torrential rain had turned the battlefield into a quagmire. Monash had little time to prepare for the November 6 attack, and his request for a postponement was refused. The Third Division lost heavily. "Our men are being put into the hottest fighting and sacrificed in harebrained schemes…and there is no-one in the War Cabinet to lift a finger in protest," Monash wrote to his wife on October 18.

Yet Monash got on well with the architect of the Ypres offensive, Field Marshal Sir Douglas Haig. He considered the Australian "a clear-headed, determined commander" who thought of every detail and, in his diary, gave him perhaps the greatest volume of unmitigated approval of any one man. Monash's respect for the commander in chief was based on the way he bore his weighty responsibilities, rather than his intellect. Indeed, he considered Haig to be "quite out of his depth" technically. The Western Front confirmed what Monash had realized before the war and what Haig and his colleagues had trouble grasping after it began—that the human qualities of morale, discipline, and an offensive spirit, which governed the British approach to warfare pre-1914, could not by themselves defeat sophisticated military technology. It had to be countered by technology, as well. The hard-pressed infantry, wrote Monash, would benefit most if its "true role was not to expend itself upon heroic physical effort…but to advance under the maximum possible protection of the maximum possible array of mechanical resources… guns, machine guns, tanks, mortars and airplanes…to be relieved as far as possible of the obligation to fight [its] way forward."

Monash's final battle as a divisional commander began shortly after the Germans' last great offensive opened on March 21, 1918. Having been directed to move his division to two different loca-

Inset right: An Australian watches as shells rain down on Messines Ridge (Australian War Memorial). Below: Commonwealth troops rest, tend to their wounded, or march German prisoners to the rear after the Battle of Hamel Ridge. Monash's successful Hamel operation soon became a model for BEF combined-arms attacks (Australian War Memorial-Art 03590).

tions on March 26, he was finally ordered at 1 A.M. on March 27 to plug the ten-mile-wide gap that yawned between the Somme and Ancre Rivers to expose Amiens. With no time for reconnaissance, the former engineer relied on his ability to visualize the topography and the unfolding battle plan as he dictated his orders from the instructions he had scribbled on three scraps of paper. Bean recalled the episode as showing Monash's "great powers of grasp and lucid expression at their best—the officers to whom they were read…recognized, with a flash of pride, 'the old man's' masterly touch."

Four months earlier, the five Australian divisions on the Western Front were brought together in the Australian Corps under a British commander, Lt. Gen. Sir William Birdwood, who had led Australian and New Zealand troops since the start of the war. With pressure growing for an Australian corps commander, Monash replaced him on May 31, 1918. Not all agreed with the appointment. Bean and war correspondent Keith Murdoch were among those who thought that it should have gone to another capable Australian, Maj. Gen. Sir Brudenell White, Birdwood's chief of staff. Whereas they considered Monash an intriguer, Bean writing of "the ability, natural and inborn in Jews, to push themselves," White was thought to be morally upright and militarily Monash's equal.

Claiming that their views were widely held, Murdoch approached Australian Prime Minister William Hughes, then en route to England. But Hughes found the opposite to be true. The division commanders, by now Australians or men who had lived in Australia for many years, told him that Monash enjoyed their full support. And White, whose conduct was impeccable throughout, rebuked Murdoch for his actions. Years later, Bean admitted that he had been wrong about Monash.

At the time, Monash was fully aware of the attempt to replace him. The conspiracy was an unnecessary distraction that could have shaken his confidence and undermined his authority as corps commander before he had the chance to establish it. Fortunately, he was robust enough not to let either be affected. For Monash, command of the Australian Corps was "something to have lived for." With some 166,000 men, it was easily the largest in the BEF and by May 1918 held a tactical ascendancy over the Germans that it never lost, thanks in part to Monash's shrewd use of psychology. He erected optimism into a creed, determining to feed his men on victory by "as far as it is humanly possible, never undertaking a battle operation without an absolute guarantee of success." The result, Monash noted, was that Australian troops came to believe they were invincible.

The key to wider action on the Australian front was Hamel Ridge, whose defenses blocked any eastward movement of the line between Villers-Bretonneux and the Somme. Like his predecessor, Monash worried that attacking it would incur heavy casualties, but his fears vanished after he watched a demonstration of the new British Mark V tank. Guided by the recommendations of his tank adviser, Monash proposed an attack in which the infantry would be protected by sixty tanks, rather than the usual creeping artillery barrage. Crushing the enemy's barbed-wire entanglements and machine-gun nests, the Mark Vs would lead the infantry on to their objectives. Moreover, using the tanks would allow each of the eight assault battalions to attack on the same frontage the Germans had allotted to each of their divisions in March. The saving in infantry—and therefore of casualties—would be dramatic.

Exhausted Aussies sleep beside a recently captured German Sturmmörser *on Hamel Ridge (left) and pose in front of a knocked-out British Mark V tank the day after the battle. With a top speed of 5 mph, Mark Vs advanced with the Australian infantry against Hamel, the "heavies" crushing barbed-wire entanglements along with German machine-gun nests (Photos: Australian War Memorial).*

Yet innovation was partly to be sacrificed to convention. Attacking without a barrage, but with the earlier Mark IV tanks at Bullecourt in 1917, the Fourth Australian Division, which would have the major role at Hamel Ridge, had suffered grievously owing to the British tanks' poor performance. Its commander urged the retention of a creeping barrage behind which the infantry and tanks would advance. To allay his fears Monash agreed, but wrote Fourth Army headquarters that the revision meant that the concept "ceases to be primarily a tank operation," becoming instead "an infantry operation, in which the slight infantry power receives a considerable accretion by the addition of a large body of tanks." Thereafter, each battalion rehearsed with the Mark Vs that would attack alongside it, the tank crewmen even taking the infantry for joy rides to overcome their skepticism.

The use of the tanks was only one aspect of Monash's thinking on support for the infantry. Prior to the attack, desultory bombardments were fired, and the resulting shell holes plotted on maps so the infantry knew where to find cover on the exposed objective. When they reached Hamel Ridge, planes would airdrop ammunition to them. Diversionary operations on both flanks would deceive the

Germans as to the real attack. A combination of gas and smoke was fired daily to accustom the Germans to wearing gas masks whenever they saw smoke. As the operation would be launched under the cover of smoke only, the Australians could assault without gas masks, while catching the Germans in theirs and at a disadvantage. Troops, guns, ammunition, and tanks moved forward at night, aircraft flying overhead masking the noise and checking the camouflage the next day. Monash went over every aspect of the plan at a final conference on June 30 attended by more than 250 officers and lasting nearly five hours. He then explained to his superior, Fourth Army commander General Sir Henry Rawlinson, "No fiddling with the plan was permitted."

Nonetheless, there was the threat of a major change as the attack was about to be launched on July 4, a date chosen partly because the commander of the U.S.

The Amiens Salient

Hindenberg Line

Aug. 8 Front Line

Armies:
British
French
German

1st
3rd
4th
Albert
Australian Corps
Amiens
Mont St. Quentin
Somme
River
1st
3rd
10th
St. Quentin

N

The Australian Corps' Advance,
August 8 – October 5, 1918

Divisions of Australian Corps:
1st   3rd   5th
2nd   4th   Front Line

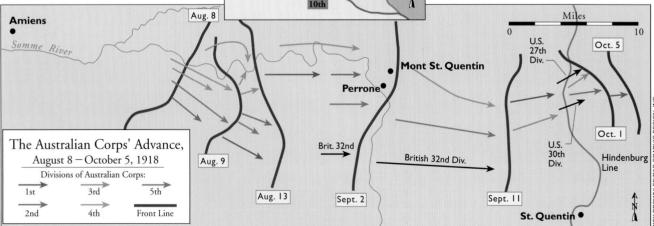

Amiens
Somme River
Aug. 8
Aug. 9
Aug. 13
Sept. 2
Brit. 32nd
British 32nd Div.
Perrone
Mont St. Quentin
Sept. 11
St. Quentin
Miles
0   10
U.S. 27th Div.
Oct. 5
Oct. 1
U.S. 30th Div.
Hindenburg Line
N

RICK BROWNLEE/R&B GRAPHIC DESIGN, INC.

Thirty-third Division had agreed to allow ten of his companies to participate in the assault. American Expeditionary Force commander General John Pershing, however, was not informed until July 2. He believed that the use of his partly trained troops contravened the agreement with Haig, whereby they were attached to the BEF to gain experience, not for operational use, and Pershing ordered their withdrawal. Six U.S. companies left reluctantly on the morning of July 3, but the other four remained, possibly due to a misunderstanding. On learning at 4 P.M. that the remaining companies were to be withdrawn as well, Monash told Rawlinson that he had until 7 P.M., when the infantry commenced its final move to the start line, to get the order rescinded or the attack would be canceled. With a few minutes to spare, Rawlinson contacted Haig, who directed it to continue with the four American companies attacking alongside the Australians.

Zero hour was at 3:10 A.M. Hamel Ridge was in Australian hands ninety-three minutes later. No battle in his previous experience, wrote Monash, "passed off so smoothly, so exactly to timetable or was so free from any kind of hitch." He likened himself to a musical conductor, coining an analogy that became famous: "A perfected modern battle plan is like nothing so much as a score for an orchestral composition, where the various arms and units are the instruments and the tasks they perform are the respective musical phrases."

A resounding example of cooperation between the various arms, Hamel became the model for the much bigger battles to come, starting with the British Fourth Army's offensive east of Amiens, which would begin on August 8. Four of Monash's divisions had the major role—to attack along the southern bank of the Somme, at the center of the offensive. Although again enjoying lavish tank support, they had to advance six miles, three times as far as at Hamel Ridge. Monash therefore planned an attack in three phases—the divisions leapfrogging between each phase. This solution would confront the Fourth and Fifth Australian Divisions with a tiring approach march of twelve miles from their concentration areas well to the rear and through positions already captured, before they could

form up for the second and third phases. So Monash assembled these two divisions closest to the starting line. After the Second and Third Australian Divisions moved through them to take the first objectives, the Fourth and Fifth would leapfrog to assault the subsequent objectives. Leapfrogging within divisions was commonplace; leapfrogging between divisions, less so. To make all the approach marches roughly equal, Monash was now proposing what had not been attempted before, two leapfrogs by two divisions side by side. Bean called the plan Monash's masterpiece: "…the elaborate placing of the brigades and the timing of their starts

Lieutenant General Monash (seated) poses with his staff less than a month before what was perhaps his finest moment. On August 8, his Australian Corps spearheaded the British Fourth Army's devastating attacks east of Amiens, capturing 7,925 Germans. Four days later, he was knighted by King George V (Australian War Memorial).

so that each punctually took up its post in the intricate task, affords what will probably be regarded as the classical example for the launching of such operations."

Although the defined objectives were ambitious, the Australian commander was adamant that they were not to be exceeded, however tempting the circumstances. According to Monash, overzealous exploitation in the past "had often led to complete disorganization and an inability to resist the shock of the enemy's inevitable reaction." For him, the attack would remain "Strictly Limited."

It began at 4:20 A.M., and was over by 1:15 P.M., the Australians taking 7,925 prisoners and 173 guns, for the loss of

2,450 men. One Australian officer wrote: "The organization of the show was wonderful…I have seen nothing to equal it. It puts fresh heart into one to see evidence of the master hand." The Canadians, on the right, were equally successful. General Erich Ludendorff, German deputy chief of staff, called August 8 "the black day of the German Army…[It] put the decline of its fighting power beyond all doubt….The war must be ended."

On August 12, Monash became Sir John, when King George V knighted him on the steps of the Australian Corps headquarters at Bertangles Chateau. Later in the month, he caviled at Rawlinson's

halting of the Fourth Army after Haig switched the main offensive to the First and Third Armies farther north. Fearing the loss of the advantages already won on his front if the Germans were allowed even a brief respite, Monash circumvented Rawlinson by falling back on a superseded order to maintain contact with the northern armies. By August 28, the Australian advance had reached Mont St. Quentin, which dominated the Somme near Peronne.

Although the ensuing battle was the only one of his operations in which quick, free maneuver played a decisive part, its scope was large enough to refute the assessment that Monash was merely a composer of set-piece battles, with limited objectives such as at Hamel or Amiens. It also brought out in him the capacity for prompt and clear decision that he looked for above all else in a commander. When his attempt to rush the second Australian Division directly across the river failed because all the bridges were either destroyed or under heavy fire, Monash sought to turn the line of the Somme from the north. Attacking from this direction, the Second Division took Mont St. Quentin on September 1, stunning Rawlinson, who thought it impregnable. Peronne fell to the Fifth Australian Division the next day.

Worried about his exposed northern flank during the fight, Monash decreed that in securing it "casualties no longer matter." At Messines and Passchendaele, he did not hesitate to bring down artillery barrages to retain ground won, despite the possibility that the shells might fall on his own men. On August 8, he was prepared to sacrifice an entire pioneer battalion in order to get roads repaired that were needed so that armored cars could advance. The Australian general's ruthlessness was not inconsistent with his professed concern for his men. He knew that a point was sometimes reached when a drastic measure would bring victory with lower casualties.

Monash's refusal to halt before Mont St. Quentin was another example. A lesser commander might have. By this time, the Australian Corps had been fighting continuously for five months, and losses had thinned its ranks. The Fifth Brigade, which attacked Mont St. Quentin with an average of 330 men per battalion instead of the usual 900, was typical of the rest. No doubt recalling his Gallipoli experience, Monash ignored his divisional commanders' pleas that their formations were incapable of further action, insisting instead "that it was imperative to recognize a great opportunity and seize it unflinchingly." As the only troops in the British army consistently able to beat the Germans, themselves near exhaustion, the Australians (and the Canadians) had to go on to the limits of their endurance to secure victory.

Weakened by exhaustion and casualties, Aussie troops assaulted the Germans on 140-foot-high Mont St. Quentin (left) on August 31 and seized the height the next day (Australian War Memorial). Below: Australian and German soldiers engage in vicious hand-to-hand fighting amid Mark V tanks on September 29, in Will Longstaff's Breaking the Hindenburg Line.

Clever tactics and massive materiel support could partly offset the manpower shortfalls and fatigue. "So long as battalions have thirty Lewis guns," Monash said, "it doesn't very much matter what else they have." Supporting the Fifth Brigade's attack were five field and four heavy artillery brigades—an overwhelming concentration. And Monash was as tired as any of his men. His chief of staff observed that he "became very thin, the skin hung loosely on his face. His characteristic attitude was one of deep thought. With his head carried slightly forward, he would ride in his car for long periods in silence."

After taking the Hindenburg Outpost Line on September 18, the First and Fourth Australian Divisions were relieved by the Twenty-Seventh and Thirtieth U.S. Divisions, which joined the remaining Australian divisions for their last major operation, the breaching of the Hindenburg Line itself, on September 29. The less-experienced Americans would attack first, taking the main German line in a standard set-piece attack before the Australians passed through them with tanks and mobile artillery for the more complicated open-warfare assault on the reserve

line. But when the Twenty-Seventh Division was checked on the northern flank, Monash vacillated before switching the weight of the attack to the south, where the Thirtieth Division had enjoyed more success.

Although the Australian commander eventually won the day, he lacked a feel for the fight. Even after Maj. Gen. John Gellibrand, one of his divisional commanders, had gone forward to confirm that the Twenty-Seventh Division had been stalled for several hours, Monash claimed that its attack was progressing steadily. By contrast, he never left his own headquarters. The reason for staying put was not a lack of courage. "Everybody knows where to get me, at a moment's notice, for immediate discussion or reference, and rapid decision," he explained. "I can have before me, all the time, a complete and not a partial picture of what is going on, and I can, at all times, reach every possible subordinate…with the minimum of delay."

Monash thus again relied on his creative imagination, applying it to maps, aerial photographs, and incoming reports to follow the battle. This approach normally worked well for him. A senior British officer recalled that "Monash would tell you which duck-board needed repairing, but never in his life went near a front-line trench." But the Hindenburg Line showed that a commander had to be prepared to grip his battle on the field itself once his plan unraveled. The other Australian commanders shared that view, and some died because of it.

They held Monash in high esteem, nonetheless. The prickly Gellibrand spoke for his colleagues when he said, "I could admire and follow him with comfort and pleasure." So could his men. As Bean wrote, they "went into action feeling that whatever might lie ahead, at least everything was right behind them." Twenty-Seventh Divison commander Maj. Gen. John F. O'Ryan expressed it another way: "The rough and ready fighting spirit of the Australians had become refined by an experienced battle technique supported by staff work of the highest order." O'Ryan had identified the twin strengths of the Australian Corps. Its quality was superb—French Marshal Ferdinand Foch called the Australian infantry "shock troops of the first order." In this sense, Monash was

lucky. But the corps' success owed just as much to his skill as its commander.

Though not infallible, Monash understood the ingredients of battle right down to the part played by the individual infantry soldier. The open mind, robustness, intellect, and creative imagination evident in his prewar civil and military careers were sharpened by three years' fighting on Gallipoli and at the Western Front before he became corps commander. By then, his ideas on fighting were developed and fully proven.

Monash's technical mastery of all arms and tactics, particularly surprise and deception, was unsurpassed among his contemporaries, and he attached equal weight to logistics. Under Monash, the cooperation and coordination between the Australian formations and the arms supporting them were probably not equaled anywhere in the BEF. His open-minded and adventurous use of all available arms to assist the infantry was particularly striking. All these things, together with Monash's intuitive grasp of his men's psychology, preserved the Australian troops' morale even when exhaustion loomed. It was as appropriate as it was fortunate that the Australian Corps should throw up such a man to command it in its last and greatest battles.

For all the fame that it brought him, Monash found nothing glorious in war. "From the start," he wrote, "its horrors, its ghastly inefficiency, its unspeakable cruelty and misery, have always appalled me." He returned to civilian life when the fighting was over. But in the saddest of ironies, peace brought immediate tragedy. His wife had hidden from him that she had cancer, and she died two months after his return home. Nor did peace bring rest. As chairman of the infant State Electricity Commission of Victoria, Monash spent many of his remaining years planning and supervising the development of the state's power scheme, his greatest engineering project. At age sixty-six, Australia's most distinguished soldier died on October 8, 1931.

PETER A. PEDERSEN served as a strategic adviser to the Australian prime minister before commanding an infantry battalion. He is the author of *Monash as Military Commander* (Melbourne, 1985).

Princely Toys

by Jeffrey S. Murray

For a century and a half French military engineers built complex models of fortified towns, such as this 1702 model of Mont-Saint-Michel showing the gothic abbey in intricate detail.

Louis XIV's collection of meticulously crafted models of cities offers modern historians a unique perspective on long-vanished urban landscapes.

"There is nothing which represents a place more perfectly than…a model in pewter, plaster or some other solid material," declared the great military theoretician Allain Manesson Mallet in his famous treatise, *Les Travaux de Mars ou l'Art de la Guerre (The Work of Mars or The Art of War)*, which was published at the peak of King Louis XIV's reign. Mallet is credited with having introduced model-building to France in 1663, when he presented the French monarch with a *plan en relief* of Pignerol, an important fortified town in the Piedmont, then part of France.

Although the idea of representing a city's complex defense system in a three-dimensional scale model may have been new to the French royal court, architects and engineers elsewhere in Europe had been making models for nearly two centuries. Even Mallet himself admitted that he did not come up with the idea for his model of Pignerol on his own but got it from an unnamed Italian engineer.

Medieval architects probably built Europe's first models. They are thought to have used them to coordinate the construction of their large and complicated cathedrals. It did not take long for sixteenth-century military engineers to follow this precedent and prepare models of entire cities.

As early as 1529, for example, Pope Clement VII kept a cork model of Florence in his private quarters while he undertook his highly successful siege of the city. The model took secret agents working inside the city several months to prepare and was smuggled out to his encampment in bails of wool. Later in the sixteenth century, the Venetians made wooden models of their forts in the Levant. About eighteen of these works can still be found in the Museo Storico Navale, in Venice. The Bavarian National Museum in Munich also keeps a small collection of five models of fortified Bavarian cities that were made in

French monarch Louis XIV accumulated the world's largest collection of models of fortified cities, allowing the Sun King to inspect his realm's defenses without leaving Paris (National Archives of Canada).

the 1570s by Jacob Sandter of Straubing for Duke Albrecht V.

It was Mallet's model of Pignerol, however, that quickly became a work for others in France to emulate. No doubt part of Mallet's success in gaining the attention of the royal court can be attributed to his timing. France had just begun an extensive campaign to extend its borders and build an invulnerable frontier. Thus, the monarch and his advisers were open to any new ideas that might help them plan the seizure of fortifications along France's borders and their reinforcement with much stronger defensive works. To assist in this endeavor, they had already established the Dépôt des Cartes et Plans in Paris. The facility, the first of its kind in Europe, was to act as the king's central repository for the thousands of maps and plans that the military was expected to use in its land-based operations. Maps and drawings were already beginning to figure prominently in French military circles when Mallet appeared in the capital with his somewhat novel three-dimensional mock-up of Pignerol.

King Louis XIV's minister of defense, François-Michel Le Tellier, marquis de Louvois, immediately recognized the ad-

vantages that this three-dimensional "map" had over the standard flat, paper maps and plans typically prepared by engineers. Unlike paper maps, which require a high degree of abstraction, Louvois found that the lifelike qualities of the model offered a realism that was far easier for less sophisticated map users to understand, a realism somewhat similar to a low-level aerial photograph. "By the magic of the art," writes modern geographer David Buisseret, "the engineers of Louis XIV, in effect, provided their master with an aerial view [of his kingdom long] before it was technically possible." As far as the marquis de Louvois was concerned, this advantage more than offset the extra costs of making models and more than made up for the challenges their transport and storage presented.

The marquis de Louvois was quick to put Mallet's novelty to the test. When he set out to rebuild the massive walls around the Flemish town of Ath—which had been annexed to France under terms of the 1668 Treaty of Aix-la-Chapelle—one of his first tasks was to have a model of the city made. Louvois had decided that the model was indispensable for managing the project and for giving the king and his counselors a good understanding of the work envisioned for the site. The model must have proved itself useful, because the plan for Ath changed several times during the winter of 1668-69, and further models of other fortification projects then underway were ordered drawn up. For the next 150 years, model-building would be undertaken as a matter of course in France whenever new defense schemes were contemplated. The end result was a model collection unlike any other in Europe.

Such was the enthusiasm in France for model-making that, in the thirty-year period leading up to Mallet's famous publication on fortifications, Sébastien Le Prestre de Vauban, the engineer responsible for fortifications in France, assembled more than 140 models for the

PLAN DE MAESTRICHT.

royal court, disposed of another sixty (because their defensive works had changed drastically since the model had been prepared), and repaired another seventeen. The models ranged in size from that of Saint-Tropez, at about 19.4 square feet, to that of Ypres, at 557 square feet.

The majority represented fortifications inside France's borders, principally along the northeast and southeast frontiers and along the Atlantic and Mediterranean coasts. Some foreign cities, however, were also included, such as Bouillon in the Ardennes, Roses in Catalina, and Exilles in Turin. Archival records show that at least three other models were also made of French fortifications in North America—Montreal, Quebec City, and

Louisbourg—but because of their advanced state of deterioration, all three were destroyed in 1872. The famous model of Quebec City that is currently displayed within the original walls of that historic fortification was actually built by the British military in the early nineteenth century.

Louis XIV's models were without a doubt important to the security of France. They allowed the king to inspect the state of his fortifications without leaving Paris and perhaps helped to persuade him to undertake costly repairs and new defense projects. At times they even permitted the king to direct sieges of enemy towns. Because of their importance, the models were guarded night

and day by a company of invalid soldiers under the command of an officer, and no one was allowed access to the collection without the king's personal authorization. But Louis XIV was quite willing to show off his collection to foreign statesmen (although probably not to fortifications experts), knowing that its size alone would tend to impress upon them the vastness of his kingdom. It certainly had this effect on Peter the Great. The Russian tsar spent six hours in the model galleries one morning in March 1717 and is said to have admired it "with wonder."

With the king taking such a personal interest in the collection, it is not surprising that the engineers—and the craftsmen who assisted them—worked hard to perfect their techniques in miniaturization in order to reproduce all aspects of the landscape (both man-made and natural) as faithfully and as accurately as possible. For example, it was not unusual for model-makers to render their churches complete with stained glass windows or to show the plantations outside a fortification with all the different crops or canals and waterways with boats tied to docks.

The 1702 model of Mont-Saint-Michel, for instance, was designed so that the gothic abbey in the monastery could be opened to reveal the interior, including the rood screen, high altar, and altarpiece. The model of Chateau Trompette de Bordeaux, constructed in 1715, was equally impressive in its craftsmanship. It was made from hundreds of salvaged pieces of roofing, framing, flooring, and walls from the actual town itself. These pieces were used to show not only the casemates, but the reception rooms of the governor as well. The model of Montmélian, on the other hand, shows the town in ruins after the month-long siege by General Nicolas Catinat in 1691. The walls of the citadel have been smashed by cannon balls and the ramparts ripped open. It stands as a strong statement to the power of the French military.

Model detailing went well beyond the immediate needs of the military and was obviously meant to impress and astonish. The "princely toys," as they were nicknamed by medieval art historian Louis Grodecki, were as much representative of the grandeur of France and the richness of its cities as they were tools

A side view of a model table shows the plank frame that was built up in places to simulate large changes in topography. A final layer of plaster was molded and colored to indicate more subtle variances in the landscape.

for the military's strategists, engineers, and artillery officers.

Originally, the models were built on-site by engineers of the Corps de Fortifications. Carrying the title *ingénieurs ordinaires du roi*, these officers—as well as most of the artisans who assisted them—were specialists in model-making, having devoted their entire careers to it. Because the technical skills required for modeling were considerable, many of the artisans' positions in the eighteenth and nineteenth centuries were passed down from father to son through several generations, thereby perpetuating the skills and craftsmanship involved. The team usually included an engineer from the geographical corps who was well versed in the survey arts. His topographical drawings, plans, and profiles of the city, its walls and strategic outer works, and all the surrounding countryside necessary for its defense were absolutely vital to the modeling team. They would become the foundation upon which the entire mock-up would be based.

With few exceptions, the paper maps and plans and the models that were made from them were scaled at one hundred fathoms (six hundred feet) to a foot, or 1:600. Interestingly, many of the public buildings, cathedrals, churches, palaces, and other important monuments were reproduced at the slightly larger scale of 1:500. By giving more importance to the high points of a city in this manner, the modelers served military officers who needed these landmarks. But this move also had the effect of accentuating the importance of these state buildings at the expense of the regular urban fabric. In the eyes of the royal court and other official state visitors, this augmentation no doubt improved the overall aesthetic

Below: Constructed in 1736, this model of Briançon, France, clearly shows how man-made fortifications augmented the Cottian Alps city's already imposing natural defenses. Inset left: A close-up of a model of Besançon's fortifications. Built for Louis XV, the mock-up of the town in eastern France is one of the most finely detailed examples of the model-maker's craft.

Originally constructed in 1668, this model of Ath in Flanders measures more than 21.5 square yards. Sébastien Le Prestre de Vauban, the engineer then responsible for all fortifications in France, assembled more than 140 models for the royal court. Vauban directed the 1697 Siege of Ath, taking the city in only two weeks.

A. LONGCHAMPT, CENTRE DES MONUMENTS NATIONAUX

appearance of the model, which for the modelers was just as important as meeting the military's needs.

Because of their size, the models were not constructed in one piece but in many sections, each on a table that was supported by a special wooden stand. The tables were fastened to their neighbors by a complex system of rods. The number of tables varied according to the dimensions of the model. For example, the model of Bouillon, which measured only 9.8 by 7.4 feet, used two tables, while the much larger model of Namur, which measured 25.4 by 21.3 feet, used fourteen. The size of each table differed according to the requirements of the total layout and was usually highly irregular in shape, with the edges following the outline of some feature of the landscape, such as a watercourse or a fence line, so as to make the joints less visible. When viewed from the bottom, then, the larger models looked like a giant jigsaw puzzle and were just as difficult to assemble. Even when workers

were given precise plans showing the position of each table in relation to the total layout, it often took several days to put a model together.

Each table was constructed like a box, with the top finished in several layers of thin wood strips, which were carved or planed to approximate the topography of the ground surface. These boards were then covered with a thin layer of plaster or papier-mâché that was sculpted by hand to render the finer details and changes in the ground surface. Sometimes, rather than using wood and plaster, modelers simply stretched a piece of canvas across the wood frame and then sculpted the topography from a mixture of silk fibers, sand, and paste. This mixture could also be colored to represent any natural changes that might occur in the ground surface or different types of land use (such as sand, rock, cultivated fields, etc.). When substantial changes in relief were to be represented—as with the ten-foot-high mountains on the Briançon model—the features might be made from layers of animal hides, which were stitched together and then shaved

to form the proper contours. Water surfaces were generally merely painted, while trees were represented by silk fibers mounted to wire stalks.

Man-made features—houses, churches, and fortifications—were usually carved from blocks of soft wood, using the greatest possible precision. Lime tree wood was the preferred medium because it had few knots. Before pasting the carved blocks on the model, architectural elements such as doors and windows were engraved or painted on heavy paper and then applied to the buildings. This technique was also used to imitate the various construction materials used in the original buildings—stone, tile, thatch, etc.—and gave the models added realism.

Once completed, the models were transported under heavy guard to Paris. This could be a complicated process, since the models were large, fragile, and heavy. It was not unusual for some of the tables to weigh 450 pounds or more. No wonder it took eight days to ship the model of Briançon, a fortress in the French Alps, about 125 miles to Grenoble. Measuring a little more than 474 square feet, the larger tables had to be carried in three wagons,

Not all models depicted construction. Some showed destruction, such as this 1693 model of Montmélian displaying the devastation inflicted on the village (left center) and its fortifications during the siege by French General Nicolas Catinat in 1691.

each pulled by four pairs of oxen, while the smaller pieces were carried on the backs of fourteen strong mules.

Transportation and roads being what they were, on arrival in Paris the models sometimes required extensive repairs before they could be shown to the monarch. Once examined by the king, the models were placed in the palace of the Tuileries, on the banks of the Seine River. But in 1706, when the viewing space there started to become crowded, they were transferred to the much larger Grande Galerie, built by Henry IV to connect the Tuileries to the Louvre. In either locality, the models were close at hand to the king, who reportedly enjoyed touring the collection on Monday afternoons in the company of his advisers.

Louis XV further augmented the collection and made a special effort to guarantee the models' safety. In 1756, for example, Louis XV created space in the Louvre for the restoration and maintenance of models already in the collection. Later he also introduced some organizational changes that helped to bring greater uniformity to the model-making process. Most noteworthy were the two offices he created in 1773 dedicated to the preparation of models—one in Lille, the other in nearby Béthune. Eventually, both these bureaus would be associated with the new school of engineering in Mézières. Each office received profiles, elevations, plans, and notes prepared by engineers in the field. With this information in hand, the specialists then bent to the task of creating the models with the assistance of topographers, artisans, and cabinetmakers.

Although models were still very popular outside nonmilitary circles, the French military's interest in the collection started to wane after the death of Louis XV. Military engineers were now more interested

in producing maps and plans that used contour lines—lines connecting points of equal elevation—to show changes in ground elevations. Although contour lines are used on most modern topographic maps, they were a novelty in the late eighteenth century. Since engineers were well trained in reading contours, they generally found topographic maps more accurate than three-dimensional models and considerably less expensive to produce, transport, and store.

Given the military's growing disinterest, it is not surprising that in the late 1770s the entire model collection was ordered transferred from the lavish Grande Galerie to the more austere granaries located in the attics above the Hôtel des Invalides. The transfer was an immensely delicate undertaking, requiring about six months to complete and more than a thousand cart trips. In the end, it led to the wasteful destruction of about twelve models from Louis XIV's original collection.

Significantly more models might have met a similar fate were it not for the appointment in 1792 of Colonel Claude-Marie Carnot as director of the Dépôt des Fortifications, which at the time was responsible for the Corps of Engineers' collection of memoirs, plans, maps, and other archival materials, including the model collection. Carnot had a special affinity for the models. He was enamored not only by their ability to provide information on "all questions relating to the landscape" but also by their symbolic importance. For him they were "monuments to the triumph of free men over slavery." Carnot's passion for the models eventually led to the opening of the entire collection to the public—although initially the viewing period was only for one month out of every year. This was

the first step in the gradual transformation of what had been the monarchy's private tools of war into one of the more unique museum collections in all of Europe.

Convinced of its prestige value, Napoleon Bonaparte preserved as well as enlarged the collection in the early nineteenth century by adding the first models in more than thirty years. Mock-ups of Brest, Toulon, and other cities arrived as spoils of war from conquered rulers. The French, however, just as quickly lost the war trophies as well as other models to the victorious Prussian army after Waterloo. Among the models seized were nineteen that had been part of Louis XIV's original collection.

During Paris' Universal Exposition of 1867, the model gallery was again made accessible to visitors—and was an instant success. But it was the Franco-Prussian War that led to the demise of the model as a military tool. The conflict had clearly demonstrated the uselessness of large urban fortifications and siege warfare. Eventually, all work on models was ordered suspended, and the models themselves were quickly replaced by relief maps in the new *plans directeur* series, published at the 1:20,000 and 1:50,000 scales. In 1927, the future of the collection was finally decided when the French government classed the remaining models in the collection (at least seventy-five items) as *monuments historiques*. After World War II, the collection returned to public viewing at the Invalides, where it has since remained as an unequalled source for the study of the urban fortifications of early modern France.

History, however, involves more than mere study and analysis. It also entails the use of imagination. And when we gaze upon these once-vital tools of conquerors, we cannot help but be transfixed by the marvelous glimpse from aloft of mighty bastions and humble streetscapes where once strode long-vanquished kings and commoners alike.

JEFFREY S. MURRAY is a cartographic archivist at the National Archives of Canada in Ottawa.

In late 1776, Benedict Arnold's makeshift inland flotilla lost a battle but forestalled a British invasion of New York.

'A STRIFE OF PYGMIES'
THE BATTLE OF VALCOUR ISLAND

by John P. Milsop

One of the most remarkable and least known achievements of the Continental Army resulted from the Continental Congress' disastrous decision to invade Canada in 1775. The failure of that operation led to the October 11, 1776, naval Battle of Valcour Island, in which two hastily created squadrons led by radically different commanders faced each other in a fight for control of Lake Champlain and the northern invasion route into New York State.

The start of the Revolutionary War at Lexington and Concord in April 1775 had triggered a chain reaction in New York's Champlain Valley. Militia Colonel Benedict Arnold of Connecticut formed an uneasy alliance with frontiersman Ethan Allen, commander of Vermont's Green Mountain Boys, and the pair seized the British lake fort at Ticonderoga on May 10. Two days later Seth Warner, Allen's second-in-command, captured the dilapidated fort at Crown Point farther to the north. Arnold also snapped up any vessels floating on Lake Champlain and raided Fort St. Johns in Canada for good measure. Shortly thereafter, at the urging of Arnold, Allen, and others, Congress authorized an invasion of Canada to forestall a British attack from the north. Some in Congress also hoped to add the province of Quebec to the ranks of the thirteen colonies already in revolt.

Americans troops advanced along a natural invasion corridor that began on the Hudson River, led cross-country some fifteen miles to Lake Champlain, and then continued into Canada along the Richelieu and St. Lawrence Rivers. France and Britain had demonstrated time and again the value of the route, which was almost entirely along waterways. The key was the deep, narrow, 145-mile-long Lake Champlain, which formed the strategic link between the Hudson and Canada.

In June 1775, Congress sent Maj. Gen. Philip Schuyler to Albany to command the Northern Department and organize support for the Canadian venture. A member of Congress and prominent New York landowner, Schuyler had mastered logistics in the French and Indian War. He stockpiled the boats, supplies, and money needed to maintain the rebels north of the border. Although originally tasked with leading the Canadian effort, Schuyler delegated the field command to General Richard Montgomery.

The American expedition entered Canada in September 1775, captured St. Johns after a lengthy siege, and advanced up the St. Lawrence River. Outside Quebec the men joined a separate invasion force led by Arnold. The Americans had reached the walls of Quebec, but General Guy Carleton, royal governor of Canada, defeated their desperate December 31-January 1 assault, in which Montgomery was killed. More important, as Carleton had withdrawn north to Quebec earlier in the campaign, he had requested both reinforcements and disassembled gunboats from Great Britain for use on Lake Champlain. The British commander was already looking beyond throwing the invaders out of Canada. He envisioned a pursuit down the lake into New York.

British Regulars and German auxiliaries began arriving at Quebec in May and immediately pursued the Americans. Smallpox had erupted among the rebels, swiftly reducing their effective strength from thousands to hundreds. The disease would kill the majority of the five thousand Patriots who perished in Canada and in the ill-equipped hospitals created to receive them in New York.

The Continental Congress had authorized the advance into Canada at least partially to forestall a possible British attack

**THE
CONTINENTAL GONDOLA
"PHILADELPHIA"**

Sunk by a round from a British cannon during the Battle of Valcour Island, *Philadelphia is the lone survivor of General Benedict Arnold's hastily constructed Lake Champlain squadron. Now on display at the Smithsonian Institution's National Museum of American History in Washington, D.C., the gondola, or gondalow, was recovered in 1935 (National Museum of American History, Smithsonian Institution).*

The opposing commanders at the Battle of Valcour Island were in many ways dissimilar. Arnold (left) was a prewar merchant who had served briefly in the military during the French and Indian War before deserting. His first experience commanding troops came in 1775. Royal Governor of Canada General Guy Carleton (right), on the other hand, was a thirty-four-year army veteran. Both, however, were self-made men who had achieved their high ranks through hard work (Left: Fort Ticonderoga Museum; Right: Library of Congress).

from the north. Now its army, defeated in the field and riddled with disease, faced the prospect of repelling an invasion by a healthy, well-trained, professional force led by an able commander. A successful drive down Lake Champlain and the Hudson coupled with a British attack on New York City could divide the northern colonies and open them to defeat in detail.

Carleton, a veteran of thirty-four years' service, possessed many of the best qualities of the generals who opposed him. The British commander had been born into an Irish family with no political connections, but he had achieved high rank largely through hard work. Wounded in action three times, he had been a friend of the conqueror of Quebec, Maj. Gen. James Wolfe. As governor, Carleton would display excellent judgment in dealing with the Canadians, his skill helping to assure that England's northernmost provinces did not join the colonies to the south in the revolt.

The American retreat had ended by the time Maj. Gen. Horatio Gates, the newly appointed commander of the tattered invasion force, met Schuyler at Albany in June. A former British army officer with boundless ambition, Gates had a talent for administration but no instinct for the battlefield. He had helped Continental Army commander George Washington organize troops around Boston, but—anxious for glory—he desired a field command of his own above all else. To this end he lobbied Congress, particularly the New England delegates, and eventually received the

The Champlain Valley

St. Lawrence River
Quebec→
Richelieu River

Montreal
Fort Chambly ■

Fort St. Johns
VERMONT

Windmill Point

Valcour Island

Schuyler Island

Lake Champlain

Split Rock

Crown Point
Ferris Bay

Fort Ticonderoga ■
● Mount Independence

Hudson River

● Skenesboro

Connecticut River

NEW YORK
● Saratoga

Albany
Miles
0   50

RICK BROWNLEE/R&B GRAPHIC DESIGN, INC.

Canadian command. Gates, however, presumed to retain command of the invasion army even though it was no longer on Canadian soil. Schuyler and Gates referred the matter to Congress, which voted that Schuyler had authority "while the troops should be on this side of Canada." Gates took second position, and both generals agreed to cooperate.

Schuyler had already formulated a plan to repel a British invasion of New York. In May he had directed the construction of gunboats and the arming of the small vessels already on the lake. If the Americans could get enough warships afloat soon enough, they could deny the British use of Champlain. He may well have recollected that a small French flotilla had played a similar role on the lake in 1758. Equally important, a successful naval defense might avert a confrontation between a better-equipped and trained British army and the smaller, poorly equipped Patriot force.

Gates and Schuyler agreed that Brig. Gen. Benedict Arnold should supersede the ineffective Colonel Jacobus Wyncoop in command of their expanding naval force. Arnold, a Connecticut merchant, had earned a reputation during the Canadian expedition for courage, energy, and persistence. Arnold's winter march through trackless Maine wilderness to join Montgomery outside Quebec was epic. His prewar mercantile activity had also given him a knowledge of ships and experience sailing them.

Although Arnold's first substantial military experience had been the Ticonderoga expedition barely a year earlier, he had already demonstrated a capacity to motivate men and to courageously endure adversity. He displayed sound tactical sense during the raid on St. Johns and in planning the desperate Quebec assault and had the knack of being able to spot and exploit an opponent's weaknesses. Pride, a quick temper, and a tendency to squabble with subordinates and superiors, however, offset those virtues. Arnold had won a unique reputation as the most effective fighting general in the Northern Department, but he required the protection and support of tolerant superiors.

After arriving at Crown Point, where the remnants of the invasion army were encamped, Schuyler, Gates, and Arnold held a council of war on July 7, 1776. The most controversial decision they reached was to concentrate the army farther south, at Ticonderoga. But of critical importance in stopping a British advance was their decision to "secure our superiority on Lake

Champlain." The Americans already possessed four armed vessels. If they could augment this force quickly, they might defeat Carleton or delay him until the onset of winter stopped his advance.

The July 7 council resulted in the mobilization of resources within and far from the theater of operations. Skenesboro, at the southern end of the lake, became the Patriots' principal shipyard. The sawmill there along with two more at Ticonderoga and Crown Point began to produce lumber for hulls and oars. Schuyler's secretary negotiated with owners of ships trapped on the Hudson by British operations at the river's mouth for anchors and fittings. Carpenters came from Massachusetts, Connecticut, and Philadelphia to construct vessels, working fourteen hours a day at prime rates of as much as five dollars per day. When sailors could not be enticed to come north from the seacoast, drafts of soldiers from Ticonderoga headed for Skenesboro to become seamen and marines.

Carleton also understood the need for control of Lake Champlain. The ships that brought him eight thousand British and three thousand German troops under Maj. Gen. John Burgoyne also transported the prefabricated gunboats he had requested. As reports reached him of an expanding rebel naval force, his own construction plans expanded. His task, however, was soon as difficult as his opponents' to the south.

When Carleton reached his planned base at St. Johns in June, he found it in ruins. The rapids that stretched along the Richelieu River from Fort Chambly to St. Johns were impassible to ships. Carlton had to have a shipyard built at St. Johns and construction materials or disassembled ships laboriously transported around the rapids. The British commander needed warships to defeat the growing Continental fleet on Lake Champlain, but he also required a fleet of bateaux to transport his invasion army. As if this were not enough, Carleton needed to re-establish order among his forces in the wake of the rebel invaders' retreat and find food to sustain his army in a province swept clean by the Americans.

Carleton's response to these challenges demonstrated his capacity for making the most of slender resources. Events would prove him the equal of Schuyler, Gates, and Arnold. If Carleton suffered a drawback, it may have been his memory of the 1775 campaign, during which the Americans had presented a very real threat to British rule in Canada. As he made preparations to move southward, he committed himself to a strategy based upon overwhelming force. While prudent, this strategy would exact a price. Throughout the summer, the attention of the

The highest-ranking Continental Army commanders in northern New York in the summer of 1776 were Generals Philip J. Schuyler (left) and Horatio Gates (below left). Their dispute over which of them had overall command of American troops in the area was settled by Congress (Left: Anne S.K. Brown Military Collection; Below left: Saratoga National Historical Park).

commanders at both ends of Lake Champlain was focused on their shipyards and divining what each planned for the other.

The Americans began the Lake Champlain naval race with the advantage of four vessels captured during 1775. The schooner *Liberty* had been seized from Loyalist Philip Skene shortly after the capture of Ticonderoga. Arnold captured the sloop *Enterprise* in his St. Johns raid. Finally, the schooners *Royal Savage* and *Revenge* fell into American hands when Montgomery captured St. Johns in 1775.

The Skenesboro yard began delivering vessels during July. The galley *Lee*, sloop rigged, forty-two-feet long, and originally begun by Arnold on the St. Lawrence, was completed using numbered frames brought from Canada. The next reinforcement comprised a group of eight gunboats, variously referred to as gundalows or gondolas.

The Lake Champlain gundalows were large, open, flat-bottomed boats. Each of the forty-five-foot-long vessels mounted a twelve-pounder on a slide in the bow, two 9-pounders amidships, and several small swivel guns along the rails. The gunboats relied on a single mast, set with a mainsail and topsail, and oars for propulsion. They could sail reasonably well with the wind directly behind them, but sailing into the wind was extraordinarily difficult for the craft. A crew of forty-five squeezed into each boat, but they could not live aboard the small vessels.

The Americans planned a follow-on class of row galleys to provide the squadron with some punch. Each of the seventy-

Most of Arnold's vessels for the defense of Lake Champlain were built at Skenesboro, whose sawmills provided the needed lumber. The craft were then rowed northward to Fort Ticonderoga and Mount Independence, where masts and armament were installed.

PUBLIC ARCHIVES OF CANADA

Continental commanders and ships are silhouetted in a 1776 watercolor by Charles Randle that commemorates the October 11 Battle of Valcour Island. Standing on the island, Arnold looks across an inlet toward Indian Point, while Captains Seth Warner and David Hawley confer.

five-foot-long galleys would be crewed by eighty men and carry two masts with single lateen sails, a useful rig for maneuvering on a long, narrow lake. Although fitted with twelve gun ports, each vessel would carry a mixed battery of ten guns. A quarterdeck provided space underneath for small cabins, and the hold accommodated magazines, supplies, and simple quarters for the crew.

As the builders launched each vessel, it proceeded under oars to Ticonderoga and Mount Independence, across the lake from the fort, for installation of masts and armament and then on to Crown Point, the staging area for the fleet's launching. Arnold, Allen, and Warner had captured a total of 194 cannons, howitzers, and mortars at Ticonderoga in 1775. Colonel Henry Knox, Continental Army chief of artillery, had removed fifty-nine from the fort the following winter to support the siege of Boston. Although many cannons remained, the necessity of outfitting the growing fleet had to compete with the need to refit Ticonderoga's defenses and to equip new fortifications on Mount Independence. This undoubtedly helped to account for the mixture of guns on the vessels and the use of lighter weapons than they might have carried. *Royal Savage* was armed with fourteen 6-pounders when captured at St. Johns, but she carried only four 6-pounders and eight 4-pounders the following year.

An examination of the surviving gundalow, *Philadelphia*, indicates that speed did not compromise quality. The builders at Skenesboro, pushed by Arnold and General David Wooster,

turned out small, sturdy warships despite the fevers that weakened the naval yard workforce and a shortage of tools and material.

As reports reached Carleton of American construction efforts, he pushed his own program forward. After unsuccessfully attempting to move vessels around the Chambly–St. Johns rapids on rollers, he directed the disassembly and reconstruction of two schooners, *Carleton* and *Maria*. He added to his fleet, after it had been dragged to St. Johns, the wistfully renamed *Loyal Convert*, originally built under Arnold's supervision near Quebec. The St. Johns yard also built a large, unwieldy, ketch-rigged floating battery, classed as a radeau, plus ten more gunboats. Finally, in late August, he ordered the reconstruction of *Inflexible,* a full-rigged ship, armed with eighteen 12-pounders, to provide the decisive edge he sought.

Carleton had no trouble recruiting or paying for workers, and he could draw on the Royal Navy vessels on the St. Lawrence for officers, men, and equipment. The governor's efforts went far toward assuring success, but they also consumed precious time. The onset of winter would mean that the lake would soon freeze, bringing movement to a halt until the spring thaw. Every week spent building ships meant one less to move south. During July, the British were concentrating forces on Staten Island. If they could capture Long Island and Manhattan and Carleton could push south far enough, the Revolution might well collapse with the union of two invading armies somewhere along the Hudson River. London, however, had already been advised to temper its expectations. An English newspaper alerted its readers: "London, September 26th, 1776. Advices have been received here from Canada, dated August 12th, that General Burgoyne's army has found it impractical to get across the lakes this season. The naval force of the Provincials is too great for them to contend with at present."

As the British warships took shape, Carleton directed the construction of six hundred bateaux to transport the troops. To reduce the number of vessels he would need, the British commander decided to leave the bulk of his German auxiliaries, except their artillery, in Canada. British and German soldiers would crew his gunboats. The governor also appointed Royal Navy Captain Thomas Pringle fleet commander. Carleton's force would be stronger and more capable than Arnold's, but it remained to be seen whether or not the British would sail southward in time to beat the winter weather.

Although Arnold was known to be an impetuous officer, faced with an impending British advance, he adopted an aggressive posture to conceal a conservative strategy. He had few trained seamen in his squadron, and intelligence indicated that the British had larger vessels and better-trained crews. An attempt to outmaneuver his enemy on the lake would invite quick defeat. The Patriot commander therefore developed a plan that would compel the British squadron to attack his own in a prepared position and against the wind. He would moor his ships between Valcour Island and the New York shoreline, anchored across the channel in a half-moon formation. Rocks to the north of his vessels would discourage an attack from the rear. As the British sailed southward past the island, propelled by a wind blowing from the north, they would not be able to see Arnold's anchorage due to the topography of the island. Once south of the island, Carleton's force would sight their quarry and then need to work into the wind in order to close for action. The larger British ships might require more time to get into action, allowing Arnold to employ his entire squadron against enemy vessels that would arrive piecemeal in the channel. The plan minimized the Americans' weaknesses and placed their opponent at a disadvantage.

Carleton's strategy played into Arnold's hands. The British commander intended to move as far south as he could in the time available, sinking or driving the Americans before him and, if possible, seizing Ticonderoga. He realized, however, as construction continued into September, that his chance for achieving all that he sought declined with each passing day.

Arnold departed Crown Point on August 24, sailing north with his ten available vessels. After surviving its first storm, the squadron took position off Windmill Point, effectively blocking access from the Richelieu River into Lake Champlain. The squadron commander hoped to intimidate the British and acquire information concerning their strength, and he communicated frequently with Gates, advising him of his situation and begging for better-trained men, supplies, and completion of the vessels still under construction, which included all of the galleys. Gates, in turn, counseled caution and offered encouragement.

Arnold, in a further effort to prepare for the British, landed crewmen early in September to cut brush for fascines to attach along the sides of his ships so as to deter boarders. Indians with British support attempted ambushes on two occasions, but both failed and the Americans incurred only minor casualties. On September 18, Arnold notified Gates of his intention to moor and fight at Valcour, and on the twenty-fourth the American squadron set sail for the small island.

The long-awaited galleys began arriving after Arnold reached the Valcour Channel. *Trumbull* joined up on September 30, and *Congress* and *Washington* dropped anchor on October 6. Soon after their arrival Arnold transferred from *Royal Savage* to *Congress,* making that galley the squadron's flagship. The fourth galley, *Gates*, was still being completed at Ticonderoga and would miss the upcoming battle.

The British squadron did not depart St. Johns until October 5. *Inflexible* had cost Carleton additional time. Reassembled in twenty-eight days, the ship had to move to deep water before the crew could hoist her heavy cannons on board. Meanwhile, snow had begun to fall in the Adirondacks west of the lake.

At 8 A.M. on Friday, October 11, an American picket boat reported that the enemy was in sight, and Arnold quickly summoned his captains and prepared for battle. He faced Carleton and Pringle with fifteen vessels crewed by approximately seven hundred men. One absence was the schooner *Liberty,* which had been dispatched to bring up supplies from Ticonderoga.

Arnold understood that the British might simply decide to blockade him in the Valcour Channel, or even split their force, leaving part to deal with him and sending the rest south toward Crown Point and Ticonderoga. He therefore took steps to bring on a battle. Leading in *Congress,* he advanced *Washington, Trumbull* and *Royal Savage* toward the enemy squadron. Carleton reacted as quickly as the wind would allow. British helms went over to face the onrushing Americans. Once the British ships turned, Arnold quickly reversed course and headed back to the American line. The galleys made it, but *Royal Savage* ran aground on Valcour Island due to damage sustained from *Inflexible.*

As Arnold anticipated, Carleton's forces arrived piecemeal. Twenty gunboats went into line and moved under oars toward the Americans. The schooner *Carleton* managed to close up with the gunboats, anchoring behind their line. British light infantry and Indians meanwhile landed on Valcour Island and the mainland to deliver a harassing fire to both flanks of the American line. *Maria,* with Carleton and Pringle on board, anchored within range of the Americans, but the remainder of the British squadron lagged. Once the British gunboats and *Carleton* closed to 350 yards' range, firing erupted. *Royal Savage*'s crew abandoned ship, and a boat party from *Thunderer* boarded the schooner and turned her guns on the American line. An American boarding party evicted the British, but they returned to burn *Royal Savage,* along with Arnold's papers and possessions, just after dark.

The gunboats and *Carleton* bore the brunt of the rebel fire and suffered accordingly. One Hessian-manned gunboat blew up. *Carleton*'s officers fell wounded, and a shot parted the spring line to its anchor cable. The vessel swung bow–on to raking fire from the Americans. Carleton ordered his namesake to pull back, but the vessel needed her sail to maneuver. A young midshipman, Edward Pellew, later Lord Exmouth, crawled out on the bowsprit under fire and loosed the sail, and the schooner escaped with water in her hold and heavy casualties.

Randle also painted watercolors in 1776 of the opposing flotillas in Valcour Bay. At the center of the American squadron (above) is the schooner Royal Savage, *which ran aground during the battle after British cannon fire shot up her rigging.*

As the battle wore on, damage mounted among the American ships. *Washington* and *Congress,* in particular, suffered hits above and below their waterlines, and *Washington*'s mainmast and rigging were also damaged. The gundalows, though poor targets, also suffered hits and casualties. One of the vessels, *New York,* lost all her officers.

Arnold set a fine example for his crew. He later wrote Gates that because of his sailors' inexperience, he was "obliged…to point most of the guns on board the *Congress,* which I believed did good execution." One of the areas in which the American crews were deficient was gunnery. Because Gates was short of powder and Congress would not send a sufficient supply north, there had been little live-fire training. Gunnery practice with untrained personnel also has its hazards. One crewman on the gundalow *Providence* died in a training accident. The rate of fire of Arnold's crews may have been slow, but they deterred a massed boarding attempt by the gunboat crews. The larger British ships did not close quickly enough to bring their heavier firepower to bear.

Inflexible fired a few broadsides, after which the British pulled back and anchored around 5 o'clock. Carleton had suffered a slight wound during the course of the battle, but his flagship had not played a major role. Neither had *Thunderer,* which had fired only a few rounds at the end of the action. The British could afford to finish off the Patriots the next day, but Arnold could not afford to stay the night.

The American commander summoned his captains aboard *Congress* to take stock of the situation. The squadron had suffered forty casualties, the gundalow *Philadelphia* had sunk shortly after firing ceased, and Arnold lacked sufficient powder to fight another general action. Fog meanwhile had descended on the lake. Arnold had noted a gap between the west end of the British anchorage and the New York shoreline through which he decided to thread his squadron. To aid in discreetly escap-

ing the British, Arnold had the wounded shifted onto vessels with cabins, from which their groans would be somewhat muffled, and had each vessel mount a shaded lantern on its stern so that it was visible only from directly aft. The thirteen surviving American vessels then glided silently past the sleeping British. The American squadron's fate now depended on the wind and seamanship.

The fog lifted around 8 A.M. on the twelfth, revealing an empty channel, and Carleton ordered an immediate pursuit. He had to retrace his steps shortly thereafter, however, because he had left no orders for his land forces. After directing them to follow the fleet, Carleton resumed the chase. Ahead of him, Arnold halted the vessels at Schuyler Island to make repairs. Three gundalows could travel no farther and were stripped of usable materiel and powder. Two were scuttled, but an attempt to burn the third, *Jersey,* failed. Arnold then directed all the remaining vessels to make best speed for Crown Point. He intended to use *Congress* and *Washington* as a rear guard. If the British closed with the squadron, the two galleys would engage to buy time.

Contrary winds, rain squalls, and sleet slowed pursuers and pursued, but the British recovered *Jersey* at Schuyler's Island. The galley *Lee* beached later in the day, and her crew abandoned ship. The British captured the vessel, adding her to their force. Pursuit continued through the night, with the Americans rowing most of the time.

Matters came to a head early on Sunday the thirteenth. As the British closed in on *Washington* and *Congress,* the two galleys overhauled four of the damaged gundalows. Brigadier General David Waterbury, commanding *Washington,* sought Arnold's consent to beach and burn his vessel, but the commander ordered him to continue. When the schooners *Carleton* and *Maria* overhauled *Washington,* Wooster finally struck his colors.

The British squadron, with the schooner Carleton *(far left) in the lead, sailed south of Valcour Island before they detected the American vessels. Hauling toward the enemy ships, the schooner closed to 350 yards before anchoring broadside to Arnold's line and opening fire.*

Arnold, aboard *Congress,* now delivered a remarkable performance. He engaged *Maria, Carleton,* and *Inflexible* off Split Rock for two hours. As he hoped, the British ignored his remaining gundalows. When he could do no more, he ordered out the sweeps, and he shepherded the four gundalows into Ferris Bay on the Vermont side of the lake. All five vessels were beached and burned. Arnold then led the survivors overland to Crown Point. *Carleton* caught no more American vessels. The action on October 13 cost forty more casualties, mostly on board *Congress.*

Governor Carleton reached Crown Point on the thirteenth, the day after the Americans had pulled out. In order to save rations, perhaps sow discord among the American ranks, and get a look at Ticonderoga's defenses, the British commander ordered the release and transport to the fort of rebel prisoners who had pledged not to take up arms until exchanged. Escorted by British officers, the captives arrived on the fourteenth but were quickly sent south lest their tales of good treatment at the hands of the enemy weaken the remaining American troops' resolve.

American soldiers pressed into service as sailors frantically row lateen-rigged galleys and square-rigged gundalows toward the battle line, in a depiction of the small but furious fight off Valcour Island for control of Lake Champlain.

Carleton, finally in control of Lake Champlain, concluded that it was too late in the season to attack Fort Ticonderoga and saw no advantage in leaving a force at Crown Point. The last British troops sailed back up the lake on November 2. The 1776 campaign in the Northern Department had ended. Arnold lost his squadron, but he, Schuyler, and Gates had halted the British until the spring of 1777. Carleton's decision to withdraw up the lake spared upstate New York from invasion, and his failure to capture Ticonderoga contributed to London's decision to give command of the invading army for the 1776 campaign season to General Burgoyne, while Carleton remained in Canada. Burgoyne's errors in the subsequent drive south contributed heavily to the American victory at Saratoga.

The American command in the north had demonstrated a remarkable capacity for organizing resources under pressure.

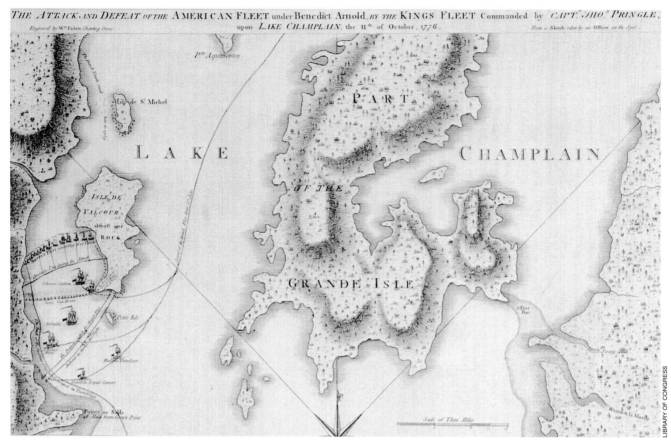

Compiled from British reports, this map was published less than two months after the fight at the request of Parliament. The line extending off the bottom left edge of the map indicates the escape route taken by American vessels the night after the battle.

Had the British been able to capture Ticonderoga in 1776, Carleton might have retained overall command. The 1777 campaign would have begun earlier, probably under more capable direction and possibly with a different outcome.

The Patriots did not rebuild their fleet for 1777, and their remaining vessels were either sunk or destroyed to prevent capture. The British meanwhile used their fleet to supply Burgoyne until his surrender at Saratoga. A few would be employed later in the war to harass Americans in the Champlain Valley and in an effort to retain Vermont for Great Britain.

Carleton has come in for a good deal of criticism from historians for his presumed lack of speed and aggressiveness in pursuing and destroying the Americans. A review of the record suggests that such criticism ignores the British commander's political responsibilities. As governor, his priority was to force the invading Americans out of Canada and to restore order in the province. He then had to assure construction and manning of a sufficient force to drive the Americans ahead of him down the lake. He also had to assemble provisions to feed his army. All in all, he faced a larger task than the Americans had faced in invading Canada. Hindsight suggests that he might have driven Arnold off the lake in early September, but hindsight is always perfect.

Two contemporaries provide the clearest explanation for what happened. Royal Navy Captain Charles Douglas, who supported Carleton's construction plans from Quebec, wrote: "I scruple not to say, that had not General Carleton authorized me to take the extraordinary measure of sending up the *Inflexible* from Quebec, things could not this year have been brought to so glo-rious a conclusion on Lake Champlain." General Friedrich Riedesel, commander of Carleton's German troops, wrote after the campaign, "If we could have begun our expedition four weeks earlier, I am satisfied that everything would have ended this year (1776)." However, the reconstruction of *Inflexible*, which began early in September, had taken nearly a month.

Carleton, the professional soldier, had faced Arnold, the self-made warrior. Arnold fought the battle he planned, made a skillful retreat, and achieved an American objective of the 1776 campaign in the north. Carleton, on the other hand, secured Canada for the Crown and eliminated the American squadron. He erred only in not detecting the American squadron through better reconnaissance. Arnold went on to greater glory and eventual disgrace, while Carleton later succeeded General Sir Henry Clinton as commander of all British forces in North America and achieved a peerage.

Naval theorist Alfred Thayer Mahan characterized the Battle of Valcour Island as "a strife of pygmies for the prize of a continent," and some historians have pointed to the outcome of the fight as a determining factor in Burgoyne's surrender at Saratoga. This, however, pushes hindsight and causality beyond reasonable limits. The Champlain campaign of 1776 halted the British and created the possibility of Saratoga. Suggesting more ignores American and British errors and the remarkable performance of Schuyler, Gates, Arnold, and Daniel Morgan in 1777.

JOHN P. MILSOP is a first-time contributor to *MHQ* who writes from Wood Ridge, New Jersey.

FIGHTING WORDS

Terms from Military History

by Christine Ammer

The Civil War both spawned and popularized many expressions, among them a considerable number of eponyms. The names of at least three generals gave rise to terms that are still in common use. Confederate General Thomas Jonathan Jackson earned the nickname **Stonewall** for his dogged defense at the First Battle of Manassas. It was General Barnard E. Bee who said, on July 21, 1861, "There is Jackson, standing like a stone wall." Jackson believed that Bee was referring to his brigade rather than to him personally, but since Bee was killed in the battle, the point was never clarified. In any event, the name not only stuck to Jackson but continues to be used as the verb **to stonewall**, meaning to obstruct or stall.

Union General Ambrose E. Burnside lent his name to a number of things that have not survived—the **Burnside blouse**, a loose-fitting shirt; the **Burnside hat**, a high-crowned felt hat; **Burnside stew**, hardtack soaked in water and then fried; and the **Burnside carbine**, a rifled shoulder firearm that Burnside patented in 1856 and that was much used during the Civil War. But his name is immortalized in a hairstyle he popularized, although eventually its name later got turned around. Burnside wore bushy side whiskers projecting from the hairline to below the ears, and in America they came to be called **burnsides** (they were simply known as "side whiskers" in Britain). In the 1880s the word was changed to **sideburns**, a noun still used for projections of the hairline forming a border just in front of the ear.

A hero of the Mexican War, Burnside at first distinguished himself in the Civil War, but after a costly defeat at Fredericksburg Abraham Lincoln relieved him of command and replaced him with General Joseph ("Fighting Joe") Hooker. It was long believed that the slang word **hooker** for prostitute alludes to the Union general. Some said he made prostitutes stay in one area of Washington, D.C., near Union Station. Others thought it refers to Hooker's own questionable behavior and therefore the women who worked in Washington's houses of ill fame were called "Hooker's Division" or "Hooker's Brigade." Actually, the earliest written record of "hooker" in this sense dates from 1845, and presumably the term comes from the idea of a prostitute hooking a customer much as an angler hooks a fish. Nevertheless, the association with the general persists.

A number of other eponyms were born, but most did not survive. **To butlerize**, meaning to steal, referred to Union General Benjamin F. Butler. While military governor of occupied New Orleans, Butler, whose highhanded rule infuriated the people of the city, was suspected of theft. Butler later gave a special award, the **Butler Medal**, to a corps of black troops for their valiant performance in 1864. They apparently were not entitled to the **Medal of Honor**, the highest decoration for valor, which Congress had first authorized for army personnel in July 1862. (Today it is sometimes referred to incorrectly as the **Congressional Medal of Honor**.)

Union commander William Tecumseh Sherman's name also was attached in various ways. Many of them referred to his famous **March to the Sea** from Atlanta to Savannah in 1864, a term that entered history much as the infamous Bataan Death March did much later. **Sherman's bummers** was the name given to stragglers who robbed civilians and plundered or destroyed property. Some of them were the general's foragers, but many others were simply deserters from either army. A **Sherman's hairpin** was a rail that had been pried up, softened over a bonfire of railroad ties, and twisted around a tree till it was shaped like a hairpin and unusable. Alluding to the widespread destruction during the march, **Sherman's sentinel** or **monument** was the name given to a chimney standing as the only remnant of a building burned down by his troops.

General George B. McClellan's name was tacked on to the **McClellan cap**, a type of kepi that he favored, and to **McClellan pie**, one of numerous names the troops gave to hardtack. The **McClellan saddle**, widely used during the war, had been designed by him in the 1850s, when he was working on various engineering projects, including a railroad route across the Cascade mountain range. It was McClellan, too, who is thought to be the originator of **All quiet along the Potomac**, a phrase appearing in dispatches he sent while commanding the Army of the Potomac from mid-1861 to November 1862. The news infuriated Union supporters who wanted to see action, and the term became an ironic catchphrase. It was quoted in a poem by Ethel Lynn Beers, "The Picket Guard," published in *Harper's Weekly* on September 30, 1861, and later set to music by John Hill Hewitt. The song, "All Quiet Along the Potomac Tonight," was published in 1864 and became very popular. Although the term died out and the song is long forgotten, an echo of it appeared during World War I, with "All quiet on the Western Front."

Confederate President Jefferson Davis' name also was attached to objects. the **Jeff Davis bow** was a wobbly military wagon used by the Confederates. **Jeff Davis bread** was a cornmeal mixture squeezed around a rifle ramrod and cooked over an open fire. **Jeff Davis coffee** was wheat used as a coffee substitute, and **Jeff Davis money** was Confederate currency. The **Davis boot**, which rose just above the ankle and tied in front with a lace, was named for him because he was secretary of war when the boot was developed. It was worn by soldiers of both sides during the Civil War, since a few standard sizes fitted most men.

CHRISTINE AMMER'S latest word book, *The Facts on File Dictionary of Clichés* (2001), is now in bookstores.

• *Robert M. Utley* examines the role of the hard-fighting Texas Rangers in the Mexican War. A decade after the Alamo, the prideful "Texians" still hungered for revenge. What an Ohio officer termed their "lawlessness and vindictive spirit," however, often put them at odds with the U.S. Army.

• *Ricardo Bonalume Neto* takes a look at the Portuguese defense of Diu, on India's Kathiawar Peninsula, in the first half of the sixteenth century. Decades before the Battle of Lepanto, Portugal defeated three Islamic attempts to take control of trade routes in the Indian Ocean.

• *Kevin L. Cook* recounts Rear Admiral William A. Moffett's commitment to the development of flying aircraft carriers. While the concept of a "mother ship" has been a staple for several generations of science-fiction writers, Moffett was one of its most enthusiastic proponents in the early 1930s.

• *Robert L. Willett* examines one of the most ill-advised military operations a U.S. commander in chief has ever ordered—the deployment of the American Expeditionary Force in Siberia. The U.S. soldiers found themselves fighting Bolsheviks after the war they had been trained for was long over.

• *Edward M. Coffman* and *Allan R. Millett* offer different views about whether Congress was right in posthumously awarding Teddy Roosevelt the Medal of Honor for his charge up San Juan Hill, and whether its reversal of an 1898-99 War Department Awards Board decision was appropriate.

• *Stephen Webbe* recounts that after a botched attempt to torch a British port, the ever-persistent John Paul Jones hatched a plan to seize an English earl to exchange for American prisoners. The results were more amusing than successful.

GIANNI DAGLI ORTI/CORBIS

ANNE S.K. BROWN MILITARY COLLECTION

Top: Dennis Showalter explains why the 1870 Battle of Sedan, which has neither the luster nor the notoriety of scores of battles, nevertheless marked the beginnings of modern total warfare. Above: The bones of Bengal army rebels litter a Lucknow, India, courtyard in the first known photograph to depict the human ruins of war. Philip Burnham points out that for more than 150 years, technology, policy, and censorship have been among the factors that have shaped the strange work and varied products of war's photojournalists.

United States Postal Service STATEMENT OF OWNERSHIP, MANAGEMENT, and CIRCULATION Required by 39 USC 3685 1. Publication Title: Military History Quarterly. **2.** Publication Number: 1040-5992. **3.** Filing Date: 9/17/01. **4.** Issue of Frequency: Quarterly. **5.** Number of Issues Published Annually: 4. **6.** Annual Subscription Price: 69.95. **7.** Complete Mailing Address of Known Office of Publication (Not Printer): Military History Quarterly, 741 Miller Dr., S.E., Suite D-2, Leesburg, VA 20175-8994. **8.** Complete Mailing Address of Headquarters or General Business Office of Publisher (Not Printer): Military History Quarterly, 741 Miller Dr., S.E., Suite D-2, Leesburg, VA 20175-8994. **9.** Full Names and Complete Mailing Addresses of Publisher, Editor, and Managing Editor - Publisher: Brent Diamond, 741 Miller Dr., S.E., Suite D-2, Leesburg, VA 20175-8994; Editor: Rod Paschall, 741 Miller Dr., S.E., Suite D-2, Leesburg, VA 20175-8994; Managing Editor: Carl von Wodtke, 741 Miller Dr., S.E., Suite D-2, Leesburg, VA 20175-8994. **10.** Owner - Full name: Primedia Enthusiast Publications, Inc., 741 Miller Dr., S.E., Suite D2, Leesburg, VA 20175 USA. **11.** Known Bondholders, Mortgagees, and Other Security Holders Owning or Holding 1 Percent or More of Total Amount of Bonds, Mortgages or Other Securities: None. **13.** Publication Title: Military History Quarterly. **14.** Issue Date for Circultion Data Below: FALL 2001. **15.** Extent and Nature of Circulation. **a.** Total Number of Copies (Net press run) The average number copies each issue during preceding 12 months was 47,498. The number of single issue published nearest to filing date was 47,900. **b.** Paid and/or Requested Circulation **(1)** Paid/Requested Outside-County Mail Subscriptions Stated on Form 3541 (Include advertiser's proof and exchange copies). The average number copies each issue during preceding 12 months was 17,462. The number copies single issue published nearest to filing date was 17,695. **(2)** Paid In-County Subscriptions Stated on Form 3541 (Includes advertiser's proof and exchange copies). The average number copies each issue during preceding 12 months was 0. The number copies single issue published nearest to filing date was 0. **(3)** Sales Through Dealers and Carriers, Street Vendors, Counter Sales, and Other Non-USPS Paid Distribution. The average number copies each issue during preceding 12 months was13,437. The number copies single issue published nearest to filing date was 13,592. **(4)** Other Classes Mailed Through the USPS The average number copies each issue during preceding 12 months was 0. The number copies single issue published nearest to filing date was 0. **c.** Total Paid and/or Requested Circulation [Sum of 15b 1, 2, 3 & 4]. The average number copies each issue during preceding 12 months was 30,899. The number copies single issue published nearest to filing date was 31,287. **d.** Free Distribution by Mail (Samples, Complimentary and other free). **(1)** Outside County as Stated on Form 3541. The average number copies each issue during preceding 12 months was 11. The number copies single issue published nearest to filing date was 17. **(2)** In-County as Stated on Form 3541. The average number copies each issue during preceding 12 months was 0. The number copies single issue published nearest to filing date was 0. **(3)** Other Classes Mailed Through the USPS. The average number copies each issue during preceding 12 months was 0. The number copies single issue published nearest to filing date was 0. **e.** Free Distribution Outside the Mail (Carriers of other means). The average number copies each issue during preceding 12 months was 1,940. The number copies single issue published nearest to filing date was 1,897. **f.** Total Free Distribution (Sum of 15d and 15e). The average number copies each issue during preceding 12 months was 1,951. The number copies single issue published nearest to filing date was 1,914. **g.** Total Distribution (Sum of 15c and 15f). The average number copies each issue during preceding 12 months was 32,850. The number copies single issue published nearest to filing date was 33,201. **h.** Copies not Distributed. The average number copies each issue during preceding 12 months was 14,630. The number copies single issue published nearest to filing date was 14,682. **I.** Total (Sum of 15g and 15h). The average number copies each issue during preceding 12 months was 47,498. The number copies single issue published nearest to filing date was 47,883. **j.** Percent Paid and/or Requested Circulation. The average number copies each issue during preceding 12 months was 94.06%. The number copies single issue published nearest to filing date was 94.24%. **16.** Publication of Statement of Ownership - Will be printed in the Winter 2002 issue of this publication. **17.** I certify that all information furnished on this form is true and complete. Signature and title of Editor, Publisher, Business Manager, or Owner - Steve Pippin, Consumer Marketing Director, 9/17/01.

MHQ BACK ISSUES
— SPECIAL LIMITED TIME OFFER —

YOU CAN PURCHASE BACK ISSUES for **$15** each or **$12.50** each with orders of 4 or more, plus shipping. This is a great time to add to your library of *MHQ* issues, and make your collection complete. NOTE: We've highlighted articles and authors in past issues which relate to those in the current issue.

Refer to the comprehensive listing of issues and articles on the following pages. Then fill out the order form inside. Detach at the dotted line, fold, seal with tape, and mail. If enclosing a check be sure to tape the bottom and sides. If you prefer, you may fax us your credit card order. (See inside)

MHQ PROTECTIVE SLIPCASES Custom-printed for MHQ subscribers! Organize your back issues of MHQ with these handsome cases. Each holds a year's issues, and the covering is attractively stamped with gold foil on black. One to four cases —$5 each; five or more cases— $4 each. Add $1 shipping per slipcase.

MHQ BI05

IMPORTANT NOTICE

Articles in this listing of *MHQ* BACK ISSUES which relate to stories in the current issue of *MHQ* are highlighted in color.

AUTUMN 1988
Volume 1, Number 1

An Empty Ocean
by John Keegan

McClellan vs. Lee: The Seven-Day Trial
by Stephen W. Sears

Why the Armada Failed
by Geoffrey Parker

If the Armada Had Landed
by Colin Martin and Geoffrey Parker

The General, At Ease: An Interview with Westmoreland
by Laura Palmer

The Roman Killing Machine
by Robert L. O'Connell

Joint Plan Red
by Thaddeus Holt

A Short History of the Management of Violence
by Martin Van Creveld

The Tunnels of Hill 60
by Robert Cowley

Alexander in India: The Battle at the Edge of the Earth
by Arther Ferrill

Britain's Finest Hour: Artists as Witnesses
by Ken McCormick and Hamilton Darby Perry

Mutiny on the Potemkin
by Elihu Rose

Last Stand
by Robert M. Utley

In Review: Vann's Private War
by Geoffrey C. Ward

WINTER 1989
Volume 1, Number 2

Sweet Wine at Last
by Richard Severo and Lewis Milford

The First Spanish Civil War
by Lawrence Malkin

The Athenian Century
by Chester G. Starr

Stalking the Nana Sahib
by Andrew Ward

Vauban
by John A. Lynn

The Fokker Menace
by Michael Spick

Conscripting the Queens
by John Maxtone-Graham

King David's Wars
by Norman Kotker

A Very Long Night at Cam Lo
by Ronald H. Spector

A Love Affair with Uniforms
by Susan Hack

Jutland
by John Keegan

The Life and Hard Times of the Crossbow
by Robert L. O'Connell

In Review: Civil War and Nuclear War
by Geoffrey C. Ward

SPRING 1989
Volume 1, Number 3

The Origins of War
by Robert L. O'Connell

Not Strategy, Not Tactics
by Victor Davis Hanson

The Bulge
by Stephen E. Ambrose

The Ineffable Union of Man and Horse
by David Quammen

En Avant!
by Ira Meistrich

Civil War Cavalry: Missed Opportunities
by Paddy Griffith

The Pequot Massacres
by Neil Asher Silberman

Intimidation by Reputation
by Byron Farwell

Gamblers on the Turkish Brink
by David Fromkin

"The Man of Silence"
by Caleb Carr

In Praise of the F4U
by Geoffrey Norman

The Strategic View: Why Air Forces Do Not Understand Strategy
by Williamson Murray

Arms and Men: The Wizards of German Weaponry
by Robert L. O'Connell

Tactical Exercises: From Drill Field to Battlefield
by Jay Luvaas

In Review: Passage to Jutland
by Ronald Spector

Experience of War: Xenophon on a Hoplite Battle

SUMMER 1989
Volume 1, Number 4

Guernica: Death in the Afternoon
by David Clay Large

What Took the North So Long?
by Williamson Murray

Bill, Willie, and Joe
by David Lamb

Attila at Châlons
by Arther Ferrill

The Cowpens
by Thomas Fleming

The Secrets of Overlord
by Stephen E. Ambrose

The Sans-Culotte Solution
by John A. Lynn

Taking up the Gun
by Geoffrey Parker

Albert and the Yser
by Robert Cowley

The End in North Africa
by Hans von Luck

SPRING 1998

SPRING 1998

▼ Fold Here ▼ If enclosing a check, tape the bottom and sides

Name_____

Address_____

City/State/Zip_____

MHQ BI05

PLEASE
AFFIX
NECESSARY
POSTAGE

MHQ

THE QUARTERLY JOURNAL
OF MILITARY HISTORY

PO Box 1539, Dept. UG4C
Fort Lee, NJ 07024 - 1539

WINTER 1999

WINTER 1999

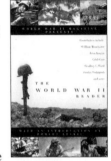